FOREVER WILD PARENTING

HOW NATURE CAN TEACH YOUR CHILDREN LIFE'S MOST IMPORTANT LESSONS

Laura T. Blind

LAURA TYLER BLIND & LAUREN BLIND BONTRAGER

Lauren B. Bontrager

LB²
PUBLISHING

South Carolina

For information about this title or to order other books and/or electronic media, contact the publisher:
LB² Publishing
810 E. Main Street, Suite I #101, Laurens, SC 29360
www.LB2publishing.com
info@LB2publishing.com

Library of Congress Control Number: 2013902363

ISBN: 978-0-9889227-7-8

Printed in the United States of America

Cover and Interior design: 1106 Design

Editor: Mary Calvez

What others are saying about this book

Getting a child to soccer, football, baseball, dance, cheerleading, tennis, and basketball, are all part of a parent's life these days. We do a great job of juggling schedules, carpooling, and being two or three places at once. Where we have not done such a good job is connecting our children to nature. This book may help the reader bridge that gap and allow a child to learn all that nature has to offer. There are so many lessons to learn—some by just watching and some by getting down into the creek and capturing crayfish. I encourage you to read this book and get outside!

—DON WINSLOW
DEPUTY DIRECTOR FOR OUTREACH AND SUPPORT SERVICES
SOUTH CAROLINA DEPARTMENT OF NATURAL RESOURCES

Forever Wild Parenting is unlike most any book on raising children you'll ever read. While the advice is familiar and consistent with what I myself have written about, the context is a wholesome adventure into leading your children into life's experiences. This book will put you in the woods or on the farm to see through the eyes of someone who wants their child to see the value of living and to have their heart race in the course to those lessons. If you are wild enough as a parent to make it through "Deuce" then you should be ready for what this book has to say about Wild Parenting.

—DANNY SILK
AUTHOR OF *LOVING YOUR KIDS ON PURPOSE*

Outdoor enthusiast, educator, and mother-hen rolled into a ball of energy—that's the Laura Blind I know from her years directing activities at Playcard Environmental Education Center in Horry County, SC.

This wonderful facility's existence is owed to the late James Blanton. His vision for educating the people of Horry County was legendary, from his involvement with the county school system to the creation of what is now Coastal Carolina University.

Though secondary and post-secondary education was important to James Blanton, his vision to teach something much more basic may be his best, and most lasting legacy.

At Playcard youth, mostly, and adults were offered an opportunity to learn the background of the land, and the very story of life as it has transpired in the black swamp of South Carolina.

It was Laura, in the beginning, who brought James' vision to life for countless thousands of school children, and thousands more who took advantage of the annual SwampFest celebration at Playcard.

Though she's long since moved on from Playcard, the outdoor enthusiast, educator, and mother-hen is evident in *Forever Wild Parenting,* co-authored with Lauren B. Bontrager, a certified wellness coach and health education specialist.

What they have created is a wonderful how-to book on living. Parents will find wonderful real-life lessons they can share with children of all ages, and tips on making those lessons real, and personal, through educational and inspirational activities.

It's an easy read that will touch your heart and make you smile, parent or not.

—DEUCE NIVEN
GENERAL MANAGER/EDITOR, TABOR-LORIS TRIBUNE

Laura Blind is a true gift and an inspiration. I served on the Board of the Joe Adair Outdoor Education Center when Laura was the Director. The school children experienced the outdoors through wonderful scavenger hunts and fun nature walks identifying trees, birds, and wildflowers. They learned to give back to their community through service. They learned the importance of clean air and water and the impact of pollution on our world. They learned to appreciate their ancestors who had carved out an existence in the Back Country through living pioneer life in the log cabin at the Center. Laura taught the adults about land trusts as a way of saving some of the special places and was instrumental in my decision to place land under conservation easement so that generations to come may experience forests and creeks and fields undisturbed. Laura's message to parents of giving their children the gift of appreciating nature is so important to their peace of mind and well-being. God placed Adam and Eve in a garden, the perfect home. This book can help families enjoy and experience this beauty and hopefully to become good stewards of it.

—DIANNE CULBERTSON
PRESIDENT, GRAY COURT-OWINGS HISTORICAL SOCIETY
UPSTATE FOREVER LAND CONSERVATION CHAMPION 2009
COLONIAL DAMES XVII CENTURY COMMUNITY SERVICE AWARD 2012

These intriguing stories linking nature with family and spiritual lessons would not let me put this book down. Lauren and Laura draw on three generations of being in the out-of-doors to deliver an important message to all of us—create and discover experiences in nature to enrich your lives. Encounters in nature have led them to deeper family connections with more life understandings. I believe our lives will only be richer by reading and practicing these principles! I highly recommend this to you to inspire your own "wildness" within your family.

—CINDY SKELTON
CAMP PROGRAM DIRECTOR, CAMP LA VIDA

Forever Wild Parenting arrives at a time when the plea for re-introducing outdoor life to the technology-driven generation is on the rise. As one who spent the first 8 years of his life shepherding farm animals and tilling the land in rural Ethiopia, I welcome the contribution of this book. Now as I shepherd and challenge CHAMPS youth toward building harmony with nature, this book becomes indispensable. It compels the reader to internalize the unfathomable, life-giving beauty and sacredness of the Earth. The closer the young child comes to experiencing and knowing nature, the more ingredients he/she collects for building harmony between man and nature.

—JERMAN DISASA
DIRECTOR OF CHAMPS AND PROFESSOR OF EDUCATION
PRESBYTERIAN COLLEGE, CLINTON, SC

Told with humor and honesty, the stories in *Forever Wild Parenting* illustrate how experience in the natural world can help build strong family bonds and instill joy and confidence in children.

—RICHARD LOUV
AUTHOR OF *THE NATURE PRINCIPLE* AND *LAST CHILD IN THE WOODS*
CHILDREN & NATURE NETWORK, FOUNDING CHAIRMAN

About the Book

L IFE YEARNS for a wild partaker. Few actually dive into the current and swim to the other side. Many simply sit on the beach and watch the tide come in.

The problem with sitting on the beach and watching the tide is that you never know the thrill of successfully battling your way through the fight or what the rush of the current feels like. Victory and triumph lose their significance in the spectator life.

Forever Wild Parenting takes you into the current and lets you feel the surge of excitement around you. As a mother-daughter team, Twig and Lauren's heart-gripping real life stories reveal how one family took the road less traveled and how it has made all the difference in their connection, friendship, and bond.

Step into the unforgettable adventures and be inspired to create your own forever wild experiences with the youngsters in your family. Discover how to put unstructured, meaningful play back into your children's day-to-day life. You'll learn to spot the "teachable moments" from a mile away and will begin to create the pristine learning environments for your children to experientially retain the wisdom that is theirs for the taking. Best of all, you'll watch your children develop into the adults you have dreamed they'd become, through an unhindered exposure to life's natural lessons.

Activities at the end of each chapter provide you the tools and inspiration to create your own forever wild experiences with your family. Through her "musing moments" Lauren creates the space to contemplate how to bring your own wisdom into your parenting journey. You'll be starting your own family traditions in no time.

*"We do not quit playing because we grow old;
we grow old because we quit playing."*

OLIVER WENDELL HOLMES

Contents

Acknowledgments

A BIG THANKS to my parents, Buck and Martha Tyler, my nuclear and extended family, and our friends for sharing their love of the out-of-doors with me! A big hug and thanks to my husband, Birney, for practicing a lot of creative problem solving in a flexible, good-sport manner. Lauren and Tyler were the spark plugs for us to record some of these stories. Lauren and Todd have been remarkable partners in creating this book. Thanks to all.

Introduction

A LLENDALE COUNTY'S FARMS, hunting plantations on the Savannah River, various camps, and the beautiful saltwater May River estuary were a fun, life-shaping wonderland of adventure for a child. I grew up wanting to give some of these "wild" experiences to others and decided to make education my career choice. Seven summers as a Camp Rawls waterfront staffer during high school and college were the perfect crucible. After earning various degrees and certifications I taught three-year-olds through twelfth graders and college and graduate-level education students for thirty-four years. Our family had the wonderful privilege of working with donors and school districts to provide hands-on learning through the opening of outdoor education centers. We worked with community members to establish land trusts using conservation easements and other tools. We were successful in helping property owners save pristine land from being developed. Donors understood that school systems could never build nor afford those kinds of natural learning laboratories, and they have left a legacy of land for children to enjoy for years to come.

Learning adventures have become my lifelong treasures. When invited, outdoor lovers from all over America would come to participate in unforgettable learning experiences: festivals like SwampFest, the Circle of Life parade, Pioneer Day, canoe river runs, building a Native American village, or celebrating the new births of our livestock at a Farm Animal Baby Day.

After many requests from Tyler and Lauren and a close call with my right hand being paralyzed for the rest of my life, I decided to start recording some of these learning experiences. My goal was to capture the details so Tyler and Lauren can share a few stories with their children someday. My hope is that these stories will also encourage you to find out-of-the-box ways to create memories and enjoy life's adventure together with your own family.

Surveys show that the electronic media business has been successful in their goal of occupying the minds of our young people. Some children spend as much as 96 percent of their waking hours in front of various forms of media. Your commitment to pass on a balanced, healthy lifestyle that includes a love of nature and memories of interactive, fun family times together is worth the effort. Your investment could not only help to prevent nature-deficit disorders in our future generations but could also add to the quality of life within your own family. Richard Louv does a great job of explaining this in his books, *Last Child in the Woods* and *The Nature Principle.* You can find these and other excellent reading materials listed in our resources section.

I want to talk to you a minute as a professional educator. If you spend time with our students in today's classrooms, you'll realize many of them are now turned off to education that consists primarily of teaching to the test and memorization. You can study the findings of education research leaders. They are hearing employers tell us that these test takers that our schools have produced don't have the skills to compete in our global job market. I have tested an educational practice for over thirty years and have seen some positive results. Hands-on learning experiences are worth a try. These learning experiences involve innovation, flexibility, networking, respect, entrepreneurism, and communication. The mind and the body are totally engaged.

Learning becomes an adventure. Every participant—whether student, educator, or parent chaperone—who spent a day in study at our nature centers knew they had come to invest in making our community a better place:

- Construction science students teamed with architects and engineers to build a bridge across a creek that golf carts could use to transport disabled students through trails in the arboretum.
- Middle school Montessori students built playscapes and hosted Play Days for early childhood education students.
- Biology students worked with scientists and engineers to design, test, and publish research on various ways to help prevent stream bank erosion.
- High school and college students identified and inventoried flora and fauna.
- College students created dichotomous keys for their own and other students' use.
- Graduate school students worked across the curriculum and throughout the community to research local Revolutionary War period history, gardening, and cooking. They created period clothing and learned to use Revolutionary War

period tools, games, and musical instruments all while making a video chronicling their work.

- High school, college, and graduate students found and worked with people throughout our region to locate a Revolutionary War period log cabin, number the logs, take it apart, move it to the Center, and work with others to rebuild the two-hundred-year-old structure.
- Graduate students participated in and hosted reenactment celebrations in the Pioneer Homestead.
- Agriculture students worked with property owners, farmers, and veterinarians to build and run a barnyard operation for animal husbandry instruction through Farm Animal Baby Day and 4-H programs.
- Graduate students teamed with community leaders to build a Native American Village and host Native American celebrations.
- Center staff worked with 500+ students of all ages to put on a Circle of Life Parade at SwampFest.

The list goes on and on. We worked with thousands of students each year. They were totally engaged. They made our world a better place and in the process they grew themselves. If we offer our students more of these kinds of total immersion hands-on experiences, it will be easier for them to become the lifelong learners and innovative problem solvers we need in the twenty-first century. Our sons' and daughters' journey to become a good man and a good lady will require a tremendous investment.

If you don't have a child's forest in your community, we would encourage you to acquire one and open an outdoor education center. Encourage your school districts to offer learning experiences at the centers through many field trips. Check our website for ways we might be able to help you.

From the family standpoint, I'll share a few stories from my childhood so that you can see what an experiential learning life in the out-of-doors looks like. The biggest disclaimer I'd like to add before we go any farther is that I am not claiming to have all the answers as a parent. Parenting makes me humble and very aware of my failures. I want this book to encourage parents everywhere to get outside together with their children and enjoy nature. The majority of our parents and children today spend most of their lifetime indoors. So while our "outdoorsy" grandparents are still healthy enough, we need to make an effort to pass on fun experiences and experiential knowledge to our future generations. Here goes. Relive some adventures with me, and use your imagination to envision a few adventures you would like to experience or pass on down your family tree.

Laura Blanche Tyler Blind

WILD LIFE LESSONS FROM CHILDHOOD

"In the end, we will conserve only what we love. We will love only what we understand. We will understand only what we are taught."

Baba Dioum | African Ecologist

1

Fiddler Crabs
growing up on the May

I CAN REMEMBER GOING to Bluffton as a very small child, back when there wasn't a grocery store, or paved roads for that matter. It was an entirely different world from the development near Hilton Head that now exists. Each summer we—my sisters Libby and Leanne and I—could count on two weeks of incomparable experiences on the magical estuary where two worlds came to mix and mingle twice a day. Our mom and dad were both professional educators. Growing up in a small South Carolina town, many of my friends and members of their families had all been students of either one or both of my parents. Mom took her FHA girls (Future Homemakers of America) and Dad took his FFA boys (Future Farmers of America) down to the FFA camp at Bluffton each year—a rustic encounter with nature in its primitive, wild form. For fun, they anchored two high floating docks out near the channel so that the teenagers could have diving platforms and swimming areas. The camp kept about eight huge wooden bateaux anchored in the water for the campers to row around the May River when needed for shrimping, crabbing, and fishing. With every camp, there were always several strong men who came down to help, as it took a whole lot of elbow grease to row a bateau against the current. There was never a dull moment at camp; each day was filled with exploration and adventure.

Water activities were my favorite, then came ball. The high school students played every kind of ball game you could imagine, and I somehow ended up on the field even though I was years younger. I loved all the camping activities and grew to love nature at an accelerated speed through each summer's new experiences.

The state FFA program eventually closed the camp at Bluffton, sold the property, and moved all camping programs to North Myrtle Beach. But since the Bluffton summers had become such an integral part of our family, my parents decided to buy the FFA cottage and continue the tradition of two weeks of vacation in the wild marshland we had come to love. I can't ever remember missing a summer out on the May.

As you could imagine, being the daughter of two professional educators I was raised to listen to what my parents said—the first time. Unfortunately when I was about eleven, I learned the hard way that any restrictions they put on my play were for my own safety.

"You girls can go down and play on the beach while we unload the car, but stay out from under the docks. There are too many sharp shells under there," said my dad as we pulled up to the cottage.

As soon as we hit the beach, Tim from North Augusta hollered for me to come help him herd up some fiddlers. He wanted to go sheep-head fishing and needed an extra hand to catch his bait. Fiddler crabs were some of the prettiest, most romantic creatures on the beach. The male fiddler would dance around the female, acting like he was playing a fiddle with his huge purple pincher and his small dark pincher. He would dig a hole in the mud and then try to attract a female to come inside his home and tunnel. He had a back door exit about two feet away. If she was too reticent to come, he would sometimes get impatient and try other tactics. Often when the tide was at dead low, the fiddlers would travel in herds of a hundred or more. It was always was so exciting to see how fast they could move. You'd take a step forward and all hundred of them would dart into their dug-out home before you could sweep down and grab one. Of all places, Tim was herding them straight for the dock and screaming at me to pick them up and put them in a bucket.

In the excitement of the moment, I forgot my dad's instructions.

Without thinking, I ran to scoop up a bucketful of fiddlers, tripped over a piece of driftwood hidden in the pluff mud, and landed on some oyster shells face first. When I cleared the mud off my face, I realized I had almost cut my wrist in two. Blood was running down all over me and the sight of it nearly scared me to death. Libby ran home screaming for my parents. Mom was trained in first aid and knew how to apply pressure to slow down the bleeding. The nearest doctor was in Hardeeville, sixteen miles away. My dad broke all speed limits getting us there. I can still hear my mom praying out loud as we drove. During the entire trip, Libby kept asking if I was going to die. My emotions were getting as woozy as my stomach was, watching the blood fill the gauze under my mom's tight grip.

Once we got there, Dr. Casey stitched me up and said I was one lucky little girl. He looked me in the eyes and said, "Blanche, you've got to stay out of the water for fourteen days and let this wound heal. And that's an order." I furrowed my brow, more concerned that fourteen days was the span of our whole vacation, and not fully comprehending the seriousness of what had just happened.

My dad realized that I still had some learning to do to really be able to make the best decisions over the remainder of our fourteen-day vacation.

After a whopping two days I was tired of taking care of my arm and sitting on dry land while everyone else splashed around in the river. I was more than ready to have some Bluffton fun in the water again.

Just when my sulking attitude had gotten bad enough, my dad woke me up early one morning to take me fishing. We ventured out onto the river right at daybreak and after just a few casts we caught a croaker. He cut the fish to make him bleed and then put him on my hook. I had never fished that way before, but I knew my dad knew what he was doing, especially when it came to fishing.

Before long I had a hit. We were fishing in shallow water over an oyster bed and I could see what hit my line. "Daddy, a shark just took my bait! He cut my fish right in two!" I shouted. I screamed for my dad to come look at the shark that was on the end of my line.

Without hesitation my dad came close and stared at the shark with me. He took my reel and brought the shark up to the side of the boat. I watched wide-eyed, so thankful to have a brave daddy in the boat with me. With careful hands he freed the shark from the line and looked me in the eye to ask, "Blanche, do you know why Dr. Casey said you could not get back in the May until your arm healed?"

I shook my head, still not sure why anyone would want to keep me from so much fun, especially while I had to watch everyone else play in the water I loved.

He continued his lesson, "Sharks can smell blood a mile away. You wouldn't have a chance. Remember how your fish was bleeding when we put it on the end of your hook? What you just saw happen to your fish could happen to you because you have a fresh wound."

I looked back down at the empty hook that had a shark on it just minutes before. He was right and I understood, but I was still sad that I couldn't get in the river. Without missing a beat, Dad put his finger under my chin and gently lifted my head. "Chin up, Blanche. You'll figure out how to have fun on dry land this summer. Remember, everyone is responsible for their own happiness."

"What does that mean, Daddy?" I asked, perplexed by his words *responsible for their own happiness*.

"It means that you are the only one who can make yourself happy. Nobody else can do that for you," he replied.

As the boat motor drowned out the silence of the marsh on our ride home, my mind raced with ideas of fun things I could find to do during our remaining days at Bluffton. Most of the ideas had a ball involved, but none involved the water—I had learned my lesson.

2

Brown Pelican Dive Bombs
learning to trust

LEARNING TO FLOAT was one of my first life lessons. Both of my parents were skilled swimmers, so my mom made floating our first fun water activity. The priceless floating lessons ended up saving my life—twice—once in a lake as a teenager and once in the May River as a college student.

With Mom, floating was all about trusting and relaxing. I can hear her now, "Okay, Blanche, lie back in the water. I'm going to put one hand under your head and one hand under your back. The position of your head determines the position of your body in the water. Lay your head back further into my hand and watch your feet come up. When you're floating you should be able to see your toes." The confidence and peace in her voice gave me the assurance I needed to lean back.

As long as my mom was touching my body, I could float forever, it seemed. But when she would start to move her hand after I was in the correct position, my feet would start to sink, then my bottom, and all of a sudden I panicked. It happened every time until I finally learned to relax and breathe correctly. I was amazed the day it happened and I floated without panicking after her last finger was no longer touching my skin. I was surprised to learn that my body could float just like hers!

I did learn to float, but never as well as my mom. Sometimes we would make a game out of who could float the longest without moving. You'd never believe it, but she would go to sleep, floating! She always took the lead in our competition. I would lose time when big waves would break over my face, while somehow she masterfully knew how to ride them out.

The May River was one of the best places to float because you could ride the salt water currents. The body is much more buoyant in salt water than in fresh water. We would start at the beach near our cottage and float down the river a ways. After a while, we would swim in to shore and hike back up to the cottage. Our countless floating competitions strengthened my ability to lean back, relax, and trust. It was a skill that had been built on the trust of my mom's faithful touch and I learned to do it on my own through her patient coaching.

I was grateful for that coaching one summer at our Tyler family reunion at Aiken State Park. As with every family reunion, the teenagers immediately congregated to think of any alternative to sitting around and talking all day—softball games and swimming were our favorite ideas. A group of us kids headed to the lake to cool off; we had time for a few water fights and races before the big meal.

I had just returned from Camp Rawls, where we had to swim across the lake and back to pass the swimming test so we could use the canoes. This lake didn't look any wider to me than Cedar Lake, so when it got time to head back in for the meal I hollered to Libby and Leanne that I would just meet them at the picnic shelter. "I'm going to swim over instead of hiking back."

One of my cousins from Savannah heard the conversation and swam toward me shouting, "Hey, wait for me. I'm going to swim it too." I slowed down a bit for him to catch up.

My plan was to use the same strategy I used at camp—breast stroke then float and rest; side stroke, float and rest; crawl, float and rest; back stroke, float and rest, and repeat. As long as I took time to vary the strokes and rest by floating, I wouldn't have to worry about cramps.

Everything was going well for a while until I realized my cousin was getting further behind and was never changing his strokes or resting by floating, so I swam over to check him out. He was exhausted. I asked if he could float, or knew any other strokes. I heard a panicky "no!" I looked at both shores but didn't know which was the closest. It looked to me like we were in the middle of the lake.

Desperate now, I asked him if he thought he could swim it. Another "no!"

I had to think quickly as I watched him struggling to keep his head above water. He was too tired to swim forward. Charlie looked like he was just treading water. We were both scared to death. I was three years older than him but had a petite feminine frame.

"Charlie," I said, "Do you trust me?"

"Yes," he sputtered.

"Well, I hope so because I am going to trust you with my own life. Can I trust you?"

"Yes," he spit out another mouthful of air and water.

"Okay, then we will make it together to the shore. Lie on your back, Charlie, and put your hands on my collar bones. I am going to use the breast stroke to push us across the lake. I'm going to swim forward with my head touching your chest. Listen to me Charlie, if you try to climb on top of me, we will both drown."

His face confirmed his understanding of the crisis we were in.

I knew I had to act on that moment of trust, before fear set in, so I started swimming. I added another important instruction, "Charlie, when I get too tired I am going to stop and float. That's when I'll need you to dog paddle for a minute, and then we can start again."

Charlie did exactly what I asked him to do; I felt him relax as we started moving closer to the shore. Meanwhile I was praying that the Lord would keep my muscles from cramping and somehow keep us from drowning. It seemed like that shoreline kept moving away from us.

It was hard for me to see the shore over Charlie's head, but once we felt some water plants we knew we were close. Our parents saw how scared we were when we finally arrived, so no one said a word as we gratefully collapsed on dry land. I have never had the desire to swim across a natural body of water again. It's too hard to accurately judge the distance over water.

Later in life, as a young adult, I became certified as a Red Cross lifeguard and water safety instructor and became the waterfront director at Camp Rawls for four summers. I taught swimming, canoeing, and diving, and I certified those who wanted to lifeguard. But nothing was more fun to teach than floating. Every time I would place my hand under the camper's back and speak the words of encouragement my mom had spoken to me, I could feel the camper start to relax just like Charlie did that day.

On another occasion I was floating just out beyond the breakers off Hilton Head Island in the Atlantic Ocean when I nearly had a heart attack right there in the water! A large school of menhaden swam underneath me. All in the same second, I felt the tickle of small fins and the forceful push of water move around me, and right as I opened my eyes, a brown pelican was on a missile flight course towards my body. Before I could even sit up in the water, the pelican cannonballed me, filling his mouth and pouch full of fish right under my body, so close I could feel his feathers on my skin! I caught my breath, wiped the salt water out of my eyes, and looked back up—he had other pelican fishing friends, and they were all diving inches away from me!

Thank goodness the menhaden passed quickly and the pelicans followed their trail. I don't know how long I could have made it under the rain of the bomb squad.

While floating is one of the best skills you can learn as a child and a practical way to build trust with your children, I wouldn't recommend trusting the pelicans!

3

Redbreast
unstructured play

MY FIRST INTRODUCTION to gators was on the Savannah River. When I was in elementary school, Dad was the agriculture teacher at Allendale High School and was always cooking up exciting adventures with his fishing buddies. On this particular occasion, he and his buddies had decided they would each bring one of their children along with them for an unforgettable exploring and fishing adventure on the banks of the Savannah River. It was a close tie between who was more excited—the dads or their sidekicks. We spent weeks preparing and talking it up.

Being the daughter of the agriculture teacher, I had already heard multiple dinner table stories about his friends' boating experiences on the Savannah and had remembered every savage detail. They had told stories about camping on sandbars and sleeping within a ring of fires, while they each rotated on gator-guard duty, shotgun in hand all throughout the night. They claimed the Savannah had the biggest gators in the world. I remembered asking my dad why. He had told me that the creek waters that flowed directly into the Savannah first cooled the bomb plant facilities, and so the water temperatures always remained warm, even in the winter. Because of the warmer water temperatures, the gators never hibernated in the winter and just kept eating and growing year round. To illustrate his point, my dad had shown me a picture taken from a helicopter by a forester of an alligator swimming across the river with a full grown buck in his mouth. Now that's a giant gator!

The day finally came when we had planned to brave the Savannah. Dad and his three buddies loaded all our gear and all us kids into two pickups. As we threw the last cane poles in the back, the men discussed how the adventure would begin. The plan was to hike in to an oxbow lake off the Savannah on a beautiful hunting plantation. None of us children had gotten any sleep the night before—we were too excited—so when the dads gave the first instructions about the hike, we all looked at each other and mustered up our best "go get 'em" attitudes.

The pickups rumbled and we drove off down the dirt road. I thought the ride out might be my best chance to ask some of my millions of questions. "Dad," I asked, "which wild animals live around this lake where we're going to fish?"

Carolyn, who was sitting beside me, heard and turned her curious ears too. We listened as Dad said, "Fishermen and hunters have seen wild boars, black bears, cougars, alligators, bobcats, all kinds of snakes, coons, opossums, and skunks. It's a wonderland of unique beauty with cypress trees so big four men can't reach around them. Life in the swamp changes a lot from day to night. If you kids want to experience the wild beauty at night, you'll have to go cooning with us." Cooning? You can imagine the can of worms Dad had opened with that statement. Needless to say he about maxed out his talking capacity by the time we made it to the river. In a question-and-answer competition between an adult and a child, the child always wins.

Dad continued his patient explanations as he parked the truck. When we all got out, Dad strapped a big machete on his belt, grabbed his backpack of supplies, and said, "Blanche, climb up here on my shoulders. We'll take the lead. The other dads will pack in the rest of the equipment."

As I climbed up, I asked, "Daddy, where are we going? I don't see a path or a lake."

He laughed and said, "That's why you need to be on my shoulders. Look how thick this undergrowth is. I'll have to cut an opening with the machete for us to enter. The plants are getting plenty of sunshine out here. Once we get under the canopy of the mature trees, you won't have to worry about briars, brush, or shrubs. Hang on tight and keep as low as you can."

I remember thinking as we maneuvered through the underbrush, "So this is why he'd been so insistent this morning to make sure I was dressed in long sleeves and long pants." Dad worked fast, and I was able to hang on. After what seemed like miles of hearing the machete swish through the gnarled plants, and hundreds of ducks under the low-hanging branches, he put me down on the ground and said, "Blanche, welcome to one of the prettiest sights on earth. This is a mature freshwater river swamp."

My eyes soaked in the beauty of it all. "Wow, you're right, Daddy. It is so different, so mysterious looking. I've never seen anything like this before."

"Look up at the treetops," Dad directed. "That's what we call the canopy. All the tree limbs have been fighting for years to reach the sunlight so they can carry on photosynthesis and make food."

By that time the other dads and their son or daughter had arrived to where we were standing. We all stood there speechless for a few minutes, in awe of all the variations of the color green on the enchanted floor of this ancient forest and captivated by the life that surrounded us in the water.

"Okay," continued Dad, in full function as the ag teacher, "somebody tell me why you don't see any plants growing on the ground in this mature forest. You mainly see huge trees."

Carolyn piped up first, "Yes sir, these are the biggest trees we've ever seen."

Then Dan took a gander. "I bet I know, Mr. Buck," he said, "because there isn't any sunlight reaching the floor of the forest."

"You're right, Dan," Dad nodded.

"Hey, Daddy," I whispered. "I bet it gets mighty dark and scary if the moonlight can't get through the treetops at night. Are we planning to come back *here* to go cooning?"

Dad laughed, "If you choose to play outside on a night when the moon isn't big, it's dark anywhere. But yes, you're right. It quickly gets real dark in here. We'll head out before the sun goes down so we can find our way back."

With the underbrush gone, we all walked a little closer to the water's edge and threw our packs down on the ground. Everyone gathered around, and the dads gave us these instructions: "All right kids, we expect you to do what we say immediately. No questions. No hesitating. If you want us to be able to do our best job taking care of you and protecting you, we've got to be able to trust that you will do exactly what we say when the time comes. We're going to have to work as a team. This is not a tame playground. We have invaded the home of many wild animals."

Carolyn, Dan, Andrew, and I looked at each other at the same time. We knew our dads were serious, and we could all feel the heaviness of their instructions. In unison, we looked at our dads and said, "Yes, sir." And then each kid instinctively wrapped their fingers around their dad's strong hand.

The dads knew they had made their point clear and with the understood agreement now in place, they led us farther into the adventure. Carolyn's dad started rigging the lines. Dan and his dad were busy pulling out the night crawlers and the crickets. Andrew's dad was helping my dad give stringers to all of us to thread our fish on. Once we got it all unpacked, my dad announced, "The redbreasts are on their beds. All conditions are perfect for fishing." It was finally time to catch some fish!

As soon as we threw our lines in, the redbreasts nailed the bait. It didn't seem to matter that we kids were cheering and laughing with each catch. Our dads were having just as much fun. We couldn't load the hooks fast enough. It seemed like we caught a fish every time we put the bait in the water. I had never been on a fishing trip like this one, nor had any of the others. It didn't take long for all of us to catch what we needed for supper.

Seeing that we kids were all getting antsy to run around, my dad said, "You can go play while we clean and cook the fish. We'll call you when we're ready to eat." But before we got too far, Dad called out to us, "Look at me, everybody. You have to stay with a buddy at all times and you can never be where you can't see your dad. Any questions?"

We confirmed with another "yes, sir" in unison. We all understood that this was part of the agreement we had made just hours before, and knew this statement must be obeyed.

"Okay, go play!" Dad hollered as he started unloading the cooking equipment.

"Let's play hide-and-seek," called Dan. "But remember we have to play with buddies." The mature bald cypress trees were plenty big enough to hide all four of us children. While we were hiding, we heard so many scary noises. Our imaginations went crazy. We were glad to be found and even more thankful to have a buddy at our side. After we got tired of playing hide-and-seek, we all tried to cross the fallen log covered in green moss and algae without slipping off. But as soon as the first one fell into the alluring creek, the water fights began. Playing in the magical swamp was such a thrill. Laughing and soaking wet now, we all sat down on the edge of the creek to catch our breath. Andrew spotted some tracks in the mud. So without delay we headed down the creek a little farther trying to figure out the nature mysteries: where did the deer cross? was the coon alone? and where did the opossum tracks lead?

We hadn't gone too far down the creek before I saw it. "Wow, look! There's a gator slide," I whispered fearfully, remembering one my dad had shown me before. Everyone stopped running and observed that the creek bank had been worn down by repeated entries into the water. "There must be a giant gator somewhere around here," I concluded quietly.

"Let's go back now!" we yelled and started running.

I can still remember how good that fried fish, red horse bread, slaw, and sweet tea tasted. Supper lasted longer than usual, as we all sat there in the swamp, telling our dads about all the wild things we had seen when we went off to play.

4

The .410
learning, the hard way

I N OUR FAMILY, hunting is a traditional passage into maturity, a rite passed down from generation to generation. I can remember the day my dad gave me his first gun: a Mossberg .410. I was a fifty-two-pound, nine-year-old little girl who had been his faithful sidekick on quail and rabbit hunts, dove shoots, and coon hunts since I was old enough to keep up. I can still see his proud eyes as he put the .410 into my hands. It was almost as tall as I was and weighed a lot. "There we are; that'll do just fine," he said as he pushed my baseball cap down with a loving tap.

A man's first gun is his prized possession. Somewhere between pulling the trigger and the habitual cleaning after each hunt—a man's first gun becomes his intimate companion through some of life's most intense battles.

Learning to shoot, however, is easier said than done—especially for a nine-year-old. Dad loaded the truck with old cans and a box of shells and headed for a sandy field down the road. All I could think about as we rode out there were the black and blue marks on my dad's shoulder after his last dove shoot with his 12-gauge automatic. The loud noise and the bruised arm were enough to make me have my doubts about really ever loving the gift I had just received. Nonetheless, the day had come for me to learn how to shoot, and I was determined to be brave enough to pull that trigger, knowing how much it meant to my dad.

He was determined to teach me how to be a great shot. My dream was to one day be as good as he was. With careful instruction, he nestled the butt of the gun snugly into my shoulder and showed me where to place my eye to keep it from getting whacked when the gun kicked. On his count, I took a deep breath, aimed the barrel up in the air, closed my eyes, and squeezed the trigger. When the gun went off, it scared me so bad that I threw it down in the sand and took off running. Dad finally caught up with me and grabbed me with his strong arms. He squatted down to my eye level and with a smile you could tell he was trying to hide, he assured me that I wasn't hurt. You would have thought I was a panting dog, I was breathing so hard.

Later that night when we were trying to get the sand out of the gun, Dad laughed out loud as he told Mother about "the brave little hunter." But in his jolly way Dad assured me that it was all right to be afraid to shoot, and that his petite tomboy was a great little hunting buddy just as she was.

The next Saturday we were back at it again. This time it was a real dove shoot. Caleb and his dad were on the stand next to us in the field. I had a crush on Caleb and was having a hard time paying attention to the doves or my dad's repetitious fire. Forgetting about the doves, I moved over to the right side of my dad to go talk to Caleb.

Minutes later, I hit the ground. I just knew I had been shot in the cheek. I rolled on the ground screaming as loud as I could, grabbing my face, "I've been shot! Daddy, somebody shot me!"

All the men stopped firing and looked our way. Dad ran over quickly, picked me up, took one look at my cheek, and wiped away my tears. "The shell's spent brass hit you, little lady. You're not shot."

Thinking more about flirting with Caleb than paying attention to where my dad was in the field, I had gotten on the wrong side of his gun. He had instructed me to stand on his left side earlier in the day, but when I moved over to his right side, I had forgotten about the discharging shells. I assure you I never did that again.

For the rest of the day, I managed to stay on my dad's left side, but the fun wasn't quite over yet. While I had focused my attention back on the doves, Caleb was still a little distracted. A few minutes later I heard a flutter, looked up, and spotted a dove flying right for Dad. "One's coming on your left, Dad," I yelled. He whirled around and fired. It was as if he saw the bird and pulled the trigger in the exact same second. After I pulled my fingers out of my ears, I opened my eyes and saw Caleb's face covered in blood.

I gasped. Caleb just stood there. Seconds later, our dads broke out in laughter. I didn't know what to think. Was he shot? Caleb said nothing; he just looked horrible.

Come to find out, the dove had flown right toward the end of the gun barrel and Caleb just happened to be in the wrong place at the wrong time. When he headed out to the field that morning, I doubt he expected to ever be so well acquainted with the insides of a dove.

5

Monster Shark
learning responsibility

WHEN OUR FAMILY WENT on vacation together for two weeks at our May River cottage in Bluffton, we all knew there would be no TV. And of course personal computers and cell phones were not yet an option. "Bring some good books to read, games to play, and ideas for making your own fun. Everyone is responsible for their own happiness," my Dad reminded us.

We all loved coming to Bluffton because each day was an adventure. Our cottage had a wrap-around screened porch where we could entertain our friends. My parents just needed to know who we were with, where we were, and what we were doing. Most of the cottages at All Joy Beach, when I was a teenager, were owned by families that knew and trusted each other. It was normal for all the teenagers to go fishing and then bring the fish to our cottage to clean, cook, and then eat them together on the porch. So shark fishing at night was a natural progression.

When you heard all the cottage doors shut at about the same time, and saw a gang of teenagers walking down the dirt streets at dusk, you knew there would be a fishing expedition under way soon. My dad, especially, knew what we were doing. He would come down and hang out with us at the river before he turned in for the night. There was a great dock for swimming and fishing in front of the cottage. At night when most of our neighbors were asleep, except for our friends who were out in the river gigging flounders, we would use the dock for shark fishing. The water in the channel at the end of the dock usually ran from twenty-one to thirty-four feet deep.

Shark fishing at night took a lot of preparation. Earlier in the day, some of us would go out to the mouth of the creeks in a johnboat with a shrimp net and catch a lot of menhaden, being sure to keep them alive until dusk. Others were tasked with rigging a two-foot steel leader onto the heaviest line we could find. Before dark we went through our checklist to make sure we had the large sharp knives, the rifle, and the emergency rope. The stationary dock and the floating dock were well lit with electrical lights, but you didn't want to be rummaging through your house while the rest of your family was trying to sleep.

Once our gang of eight or so had arrived at the dock with supplies in hand, we would start by cutting the menhaden. When we finished, we would have filled several large buckets with bloody chum. The next step was dumping the chum into the river under a lighted section so we could see the fins that would soon appear. It never took long before the sharks arrived.

I remembered my dad's lesson about sharks, and the old-timers always told us the same thing: "Sharks can smell blood a mile away." We believed them.

I wish I could describe what it looked like and *felt* like to see so many sharks churning up the water beneath that dock. We all got serious when we saw some of their large bodies thrashing each other for the fish. They were all *so* big! The strongest boys in our group manned the rod and reel, and, yes, it took several guys to do the job.

I remember one night in particular. We dumped the chum, and it wasn't long before we had a strike. If our buddies hadn't locked down their rigs, they would have been yanked off the dock into the swarming fest of sharks below. The dock sounded like a football stadium. All eight of us knew we had to work together to win the fight. I'm surprised we never woke up the people sleeping in the cottages on the front beach.

It took two of our strongest boys to fight the monster shark. They were trying to keep the shark from getting too much slack in the line because too much slack would have allowed the shark to jump and break the line. After a while, the shark wore our boys out. That's when we moved to Plan B. Four other boys had already started backing the johnboat down the boat ramp about a hundred feet from the dock. Once they were in the water and were secured in the boat, the two boys on the dock passed off the rod and reel to the four boys in the johnboat. They rigged the rod and reel to the boat so that the shark pulled the boat (with four hundred pounds of boys in it). The shark pulled that boat around the river for what seemed like hours until it finally got tired. We all watched, following the boat lights back and forth with our eyes.

When the boat finally stopped moving, we heard the motor crank. The boys drove the johnboat up beside the floating dock, shouting instructions to transfer the rod and reel back to the boys on the dock. "Get the rifle ready," I heard. I made sure I was out of the way.

With the lights on the dock now giving us a clear view, we all screamed when the shark broke the water. It looked like it was as long as the boat. It was definitely too dangerous to gaff.

The guys in the boat strategized with the boys on the dock and figured out a way to pass by and bring the shark right beside the floating dock for the shoot. The shark was so tired that the dock boys put the barrel of the gun right up to its head and pulled the trigger.

The gun fired one time, instantly killing the shark.

We all thought it was over. It stopped moving, and the boys pulled the shark onto the floating dock. But seconds after it was out of the water, the shark went into labor and gave birth to live sharks! She might have been brain dead, but her body instinctively and automatically gave birth. Most sharks don't hatch from eggs like other fish do. We all watched, in silent amazement, as the newborn sharks came out of her. Without hesitation we gently placed the newborns back into the May.

"Okay, Blanche, bring the knives and let's see what this shark looks like inside," Tim shouted.

The adventure had been enough already, but we knew this was our only chance to see the intricacies of this massive beast. I can still remember everyone's comments as we dissected the shark; it was an explosion of curiosity and discovery all at once:

"So sharp! Would you look at all those jagged rows of teeth! No wonder it's hard to stop the bleeding when a shark bites you!"

"Hey, somebody cut open the stomach. Let's see what she had for supper!"

"Ah man, touch her skin! She doesn't have scales like most fish. It feels rough like sandpaper."

"I wish we had some way of weighing this shark! We've never seen one this big . . . anywhere!"

"Yeah, and we caught it right at the end of our swimming dock!"

That's when the comments stopped abruptly and we looked at each other in silence with faces that said it all.

"You know what this means, don't you?" one of the guys finally took the lead to say. "We might need to stop shark fishing off of our swimming dock!"

With the thought of this being our last shark expedition from our convenient rendezvous point at the end of the dock, we decided we just *had* to let our neighbors in on our secret. It took all eight of us lifting her together, but we finally carried that shark down the long dock and hoisted her up with the thickest rope we had. We decided to leave her hanging from the biggest tree branch we could find (hoping her weight wouldn't snap the branch by morning), certain that someone would see our trophy by noon.

With aching muscles and the final rush of adrenaline giving its last hurrah, we stood there, taking it all in, speechless about the death and life we had altered, irrevocably.

Every one of us was covered in blood from head to toe and smelled like the dead carcasses that were inside the shark's freshly dissected gut. We had been up all night fighting her. And with daylight soon to be dancing on the horizon, we quickly gathered our gun, knives, and buckets and headed for the outdoor shower to clean up. We had only a few hours to get some sleep before our parents would be awake.

The next day was an unusually different day for all eight of us. It was as if we had gone to bed teenagers and woken up as wise old men. We were all starting to come to terms with the life we had taken and the dangers, the thrills, and the emotion that had unfolded in just one night. Somehow none of us felt like bragging that day.

I remember all of us "casually" strolling down near the front beach where we had left her, to watch the expressions of our neighbors that next morning. "Did that come out of *our river?*" "It's HUGE!" "What a monster! How much you reckon that thing weighs?"

The crowd had started forming, and no one could believe what they saw. That's when I saw my dad walk down the street with several of his friends—the other strong dads of the teenagers who had hardly gotten any sleep the night before. The muscular men cut the rope from the branch and hauled the shark over to a boat. They gave us a look. Not a scolding look or an approving look either, but one that seemed to say that they too had once wrestled a shark all night. Minutes later, they were driving off in the boat out to the deep waters to put our shark to rest.

By the time we were teenagers, our parents had taught us how to respect the river if we wanted to stay alive. Daily we saw life created and life taken in death. We knew we weren't immune to that constant flow of reality. We knew people who had drowned. We knew others who had been injured on the water. So, we learned to respect the vulnerability of life and the consequences of decisions.

We also learned that we needed each other, not only to survive, but to really enjoy our water world. Neighbors helped each other keep all our boats running. Each of us had developed skills according to our special interests. We played together and ate together. We got to know and trust our river friends and their families. We knew the behavior our parents expected from us, and we all helped each other toe the line. Drinking, smoking, and premarital sex didn't appeal to us—the river and the wild adventures overpowered the negative temptations. Our parents trusted us to make the right decisions and to be careful even in the midst of so many risks. We also trusted and knew we needed our parents—in more practical ways than most.

Note:

This adventure was in the 1960s when there were almost no regulations on shark fishing. Today many of the sharks living in South Carolina waters are endangered to the point that they are protected by regulations. So now when we go shark fishing, we check with SCDNR for the current regulations. We use the book *Sharks of South Carolina* by Charles Farmer to identify the species caught and abide by the specific species regulations. By the way, several in our "monster shark fishing group" wound up investing their careers in wildlife conservation. That night had a lasting impact on us all.

WILD LIFE LESSONS FROM PARENTING

"*The foregoing generations beheld God and nature face to face; we, through their eyes. Why should not we also enjoy an original revelation to the universe? Why should not we have a poetry and philosophy of insight and not of tradition, and a religion by revelation to us, and not the history of theirs?*"

RALPH WALDO EMERSON

6

Puppy Love
a mother's instinct

"GOOD MORNING. How can I help you today?" Dr. Smith inquired as he gave a good look at the fluffy white poodle in my arms.

I doubtfully replied, "I sure hope you can help us. I called your office this morning to ask if you dealt with the psychological problems of your patients, and your receptionist just laughed out loud, so I'm not sure if you *can* help us."

Curious and intrigued by my challenge, he chuckled and said, "Well now, what's got you troubled?"

I paused before I replied, contemplating one last time if I was absolutely sure that I wanted to share this embarrassing news about our dog. "My husband, Birney, and I moved to Conway two months ago. By the way, my name is Blanche, but everyone calls me Twig. Our first baby is due next week and our dog seems to be going insane. We have been feeding her as normal and letting her get a good dose of sunshine every day. We take her on long walks and let her run around the yard. I've done everything I can think of to help her. I just don't know what's wrong with her!"

Dr. Smith laughed and started examining Buffy. "Go on," he said.

I continued, "My family has always had dogs as pets, but the only time I've seen one of our dogs' behavior change so radically was with one named Bobbie. My sister Libby was about seven and I was about five, and we were playing dress-up with Bobbie. Libby had pinned Bobbie's ears together on top of her head with a hair pin while we finished putting some of our clothes on her. The dog started whimpering, growling, rolling on the ground, digging, and running in circles. My mom panicked when she looked out the window and saw Bobbie's behavior. Bobbie was moving so fast that Mom couldn't see the bobby pin, so she was afraid our dog might be rabid. After a neighbor's collie was found to be rabid, my sister Libby had just gone through the painful series of thirteen shots in her abdomen. Needless to say, Mom was most relieved when she got close enough to discover the real problem."

Dr. Smith looked up over his glasses with a scolding expression as if to say, "You did what to that dog's ears?!" I glanced back down and continued.

"To my knowledge, Buffy's problem is not physical. She is current on all of her injections, has not been exposed to any stray dogs, and is very healthy. About fourteen months ago, she gave birth to four healthy puppies."

Dr. Smith completed his exam with, "Yep, Buffy appears to be a healthy poodle. Tell me about this strange behavior you've been observing lately."

"Well, it started a few weeks ago. I was washing dishes in the kitchen one afternoon and heard strange noises coming from our bedroom. Buffy was on Birney's side of the closet, moving things out of her way and going round and round in a circle, clawing up the carpet. I stood there watching her for about ten minutes. Even when I called her name, she wouldn't stop. She just kept going, as if she had this insatiable desire to find something under the carpet."

Dr. Smith was staring into Buffy's ears with the magnifying instrument and palpating her neck, as if he wasn't the least bit concerned with my report.

I continued, emphasizing the severity of her behavior, "It's been weeks now and she keeps clawing up the carpet in the same spot and running in circles. If we forget and leave the nursery bedroom door open, she'll go in there and grab one of the baby's stuffed animals or toys and bring it into the clawed up area in the closet. I just don't think I can deal with a crazy dog and a newborn baby at the same time! What is wrong with her?"

Dr. Smith started laughing again. "Nothing is wrong with her, Twig," he said confidently. "Buffy is experiencing a false pregnancy. She is preparing her nest, her own birthing area."

"You've got to be kidding me," I said. "How did she come down with a false pregnancy? She has been spayed!"

Dr. Smith quickly replied, "You caused this pregnancy."

"What?" I replied, not believing what I was hearing.

"Buffy has reacted to the hormonal change in your body's chemistry through her sense of smell. When you give birth next week, Buffy will stop nesting. The only catch is—your baby will be her baby. But don't worry. She'll be a good little mom," he said, patting her on the head. And with that comment, he left the exam room.

Still in shock, I carried our little poodle out of the veterinarian clinic; she rested peacefully on the big protrusion from my abdomen as I waddled to the car. Even though I was completely embarrassed that I just paid for an appointment to see if our dog was going crazy, I was relieved to know that Buffy wasn't insane. Birney and I laughed through supper that night. Dr. Smith probably did too.

The veterinarian's diagnosis was correct. Our beautiful little boy was born just five days later. As soon as we came home from the hospital, Buffy had her moment of glory with Tyler. She nearly wagged her tail off her bottom when Birney pushed open the door and she saw us for the first time. She sniffed every inch of his body and snuggled her face beside his warm cheek, overwhelmed by the joy of touching "her son." He had arrived, and she knew he was hers.

Then the true test of motherhood came. If I happened to be asleep and Tyler moved or made any noise in his crib, Buffy would wake me up and wouldn't leave me alone until I went in and picked him up. When we changed his diaper, we had to take it outside and put it in the big trashcan or Buffy would find a way to clean the diaper herself. She never even let a crumb stay under his high chair. Amazing what a variety of baby foods she ate! It was like having a live-in maid, babysitter, and mother-in-law, all at the same time.

She was the same way with both of our children. Two years later when I was pregnant with Lauren, we preemptively moved all of Birney's shoes out of the closet. And before you knew it, she was back to the clawing and circling frenzy.

As Tyler and Lauren reached toddlerhood, Buffy was insistent on sharing her sock toys with them. She let them pull her and her toys all over the house. When Buffy growled, they would laugh, and Buffy would get even more excited. I am surprised she didn't lose some of her front teeth. Tyler and Lauren both started crawling and walking early, pushing up on Buffy, motivated by her teasing game of chase.

I never thought I would be thankful for false pregnancies, but I was. It was incredible to see such a strong instinct to be a mother in our little fifteen-pound poodle. If pharmaceutical companies could figure out how to trigger that kind of nurturing behavior in humans just through our sense of smell, a lot of homes sure would be changed. Maybe God just decided our family needed a little extra puppy love.

 TAKE A MINUTE TO MUSE . . .

- It doesn't take long in life to discover that learning to laugh at ourselves is much better than stressing out. Can you think of a memory in your life that still brings you laughter?
- What was it about that memory that made you laugh instead of stress?
- In light of that laugh, think about the situations and events that are unfolding today in your life. What will you do today to teach your children how to laugh through life, and see the rainbow beyond the storm?

CREATE YOUR OWN FOREVER WILD EXPERIENCE . . .

Have you ever created an opportunity for your child to observe the miracle of a new life coming into this world?

Here's an easy activity you can do with your children to bring them into the joy of creation and new birth: RAISING PAINTED LADY BUTTERFLIES.

1. You can buy everything you need from any good biological supply catalog. We use Carolina Biological [www.carolina.com]. You could start with the Painted Lady Butterfly Life Cycle Set, which includes instructions that explain how to care for the chrysalises.

2. The first thing your child will see is a red liquid around the attachment area of the chrysalis—that's when the questions usually begin. But don't worry, you really can't find the words to explain how the caterpillar encloses itself in a chrysalis while the body turns into a liquid form, or how it is transformed into a beautiful butterfly with soaking wet wings as it emerges.

3. Questions are integral to the process of learning; use your child's questions as a springboard for their experiential lesson. Help them figure out the answers, and walk through the learning process with them as they research metamorphosis. It's more fun to explore alongside your children. Don't worry if you don't know the answers to their questions; you wouldn't want to have all the answers even if you could.

4. After you observe the miracle of metamorphosis, you will find yourself wanting to identify the native butterflies that live around your home. Your children will suddenly start "seeing butterflies" every time you venture outside. An inexpensive field guide book is a great tool to have at home for identification of butterflies and the plants they enjoy.

5. After you've learned your butterfly's favorite host plant, your next adventure can be planting a host plant in your yard to attract that specific butterfly. For example, in our area we have a lot of yellow poplar trees that attract Tiger Swallowtail butterflies. Butterflies lay their eggs on the host plant leaves, which will be eaten by that particular caterpillar species. Black Swallowtail caterpillars feed on parsley, dill, or fennel. What host plant does your Painted Lady caterpillar enjoy eating?

6. About four to ten days after our Swallowtail lays her eggs on the fennel leaves, tiny black caterpillars will crawl out of the eggs. Once they start eating the leaf, their entire appearance changes. They will continue to eat voraciously and grow until they are about the size of your finger. If you get a Swallowtail, you will need several fennel or parsley plants if you raise them inside a terrarium. For Painted Ladies, you should have daisy plants, American Elm leaves, or Black Cherry leaves.

7. After about three to four weeks as a caterpillar, you will need to provide a place where the caterpillar can attach its body and build a chrysalis. A small screen-covered aquarium is a perfect environment. Both types

of butterflies like to join themselves to the stems of their preferred plants.

8. Watching the emergence of a beautiful butterfly is more exciting than you can imagine, but at first, be careful to let the wings dry. Don't touch the butterfly—not yet. (You will need to provide some sugar water. Carolina Biological supplies all the instructions.)

9. Take the aquarium outside on a warm, sunny day. After the wings are dry and pumped up with fluid from its body, you can place your hand near the butterfly and it will usually crawl onto your hand. Raise your hand into the air and cheer it on as it takes its first flight. We like to set our butterflies free as soon as they can fly. Their life is so short.

10. Life is indeed intricate and fragile, yet strong and determined. When was the last time you cherished the value of life with someone you love?

7

Red-Tail Hawk and Little Red Hen
immediate obedience

TYLER WAS IN THE FIRST GRADE. Lauren was about four years old. It was Sunday afternoon, and I needed to set up the model rocket launch pads and mark off the shooting field for the competitive rocket tournament that was taking place first thing on Monday morning. The fourth- and fifth-grade students would be charging off the bus with excitement as soon as they got to Playcard. Tyler was going to help me carry some equipment over to the launch area. Lauren was playing hide-and-seek with the little red hen and her nine peeping biddies.

I had trained the chickens to stay around the Playcard Environmental Education Center building so I could use them for instructional purposes. During the teaching day, I kept chick feed in my pockets, and they would follow me around to get the feed. So, to keep Lauren busy while Tyler and I assembled the launch pads, I filled Lauren's pockets with feed.

When she threw out a small handful of feed on the ground, the little red hen would get up to run over and peck up the cracked corn. That's when Lauren could see and count her babies as the trail of little biddies followed closely behind. When the little red hen sat down, her biddies disappeared under her feathered body once again. The laughter-filled game went on for quite some time. After a long giggle, Lauren would squeal, "Where are you?" and throw the corn again.

Seeing that she was thoroughly amused, I told Lauren, "Stay right here behind the Center and play with the biddies while Tyler and I set up the launch area right over there. I can see you and hear you from where we'll be, so just holler if you need anything."

Tyler and I grabbed the stakes and rope and headed for the rocket field. We had completed one launch pad when we heard a loud "Eeeek!" I looked up and saw a big red-tailed hawk circling above. He had spotted the little red hen and her biddies. Lauren was playing, oblivious to the danger flying overhead.

In one silent second life changed drastically. The hawk swooped down and with deadly aim took the little red hen's head off with his talons. Lauren was panicking, screaming as she watched the little red hen flop up into the air and down on the ground, with blood spurting out each time the hen's heart continued to beat. Tyler and I were a hundred yards away. I looked at Lauren, and back up at the hawk. The red-tail was circling again. I knew that the hawk didn't want to pick up the hen until all the blood had pumped out of her body and she had stopped flopping around. The hawk wouldn't be able to fly with such a large weight jumping around in its grasp.

But he was circling again, coming back to pick up the little biddies. I started running towards Lauren and yelling for her to gather up the little biddies. "Lauren, lie down on the ground and pull up your shirt for the little biddies to come inside! Hide them like the little red hen hid them!" I yelled as I ran, completely aware that she must act immediately or we would lose another one. The hawk was swooping down to take a biddy. You could hear the fear in Lauren's voice. She was afraid the hawk would hurt her, but I yelled out to assure her that she would be okay. "Please, Lauren, hide the biddies. Be their mommy!" I was almost to her now, but still desperately hoping she would respond. Lauren looked up again, saw Red-tail getting closer and made up her mind. She started running quickly, gathering the biddies in her shirt and, just as the hawk swooped by her head, she lay down on the ground, holding her shirt tight so not one biddy could escape.

Tyler and I got to her just as the hawk circled again and swooped down to pick up the lifeless body of the little red hen. Red-tail was a strong flier. His muscular legs held tightly as he lifted off the ground, clenching his meal. With my two children and nine little biddies on my lap, we held each other close as we watched Red-tail carry his catch all the way up to his nest in the top of the big white oak tree.

"Look, Lauren, there's his mate. I bet they have baby hawks that they are feeding." Lauren was still breathing hard and shaking all over, certainly more concerned with the biddies in her lap than with the hawk's hungry babies.

As we sat there a little longer, I quietly reflected on her decision to obey. There are times in life when immediate obedience is the only action that will save us. It's in those moments, when life or death is hanging on the thread of one small choice, that you see trust in its tangible form.

🕐 TAKE A MINUTE TO MUSE . . .

- How might your life be different when you successfully teach your children the value of immediate obedience; moreover, how might *their* life be different? Take a minute to recall a time when your immediate obedience saved a life or prevented unnecessary suffering. How has your life been affected by that momentary choice?
- How did you learn the value of immediate obedience? Can you see the environment of trust that enabled you to obey so boldly in the face of fear or uncertainty? What are some specific ways you can build trust and strengthen the connection between you and your children now, so that in those moments of do-or-die decisions, they are able to lean into the strength of your connection to find the courage to act?
- Great are the rewards for learning obedience at a young age. As parents we often want to protect our children from harm at all costs, especially when they're young. The catch-22 is that the consequences of poor choices only intensify as we age, problems get bigger, and the possibility of pain proportionally increases. Instead of rescuing your children from every negative consequence of their choices, or making them do it "your way" (so they

don't feel any pain), what are some natural consequences that you can choose to allow your children to experience now (while the suffering is as minimal as possible) so that they learn *now,* instead of later? Certainly, parental discretion is advised—but really, is your habit of going behind them or "fixing" the scenario or "helping" them do it right really teaching them anything? If your children don't learn the lesson of immediate obedience now, how might their life look at thirty?

CREATE YOUR OWN FOREVER WILD EXPERIENCE . . .

If you're reading this story to a young child you may want to discuss with them these questions.

- Was it morally wrong for Red-tail to kill the little red hen?
  No.
- Where did the hawk take the little red hen?
  Right. He took it up to his mate and their two baby hawks in their nest way up in the top of the white oak tree. They are a part of a food chain too. Just like the hawk family, we also eat chicken in our food chain.
- What is a food chain?
  Well, Lauren fed the little red hen cracked corn. So it goes like this: the corn is eaten by the chicken which is eaten by the hawk.
- What do we call the organism that gets eaten?
  The prey.
- And what do we call the organism that eats the prey?
  The predator.

- What do we call an organism that can make its own food? It doesn't have to go around eating other organisms. The producer.
- What is the producer in this food chain? The corn.

In addition to doing a lot of hunting and fishing, my family grew delicious food in our garden. At an early age we learned the meaning of "Two for the crow and one to grow."

- The Master Designer has woven an intricate web of life with each part affecting and in some way depending on the other. Life is not an accident that just happens, nor is it maintained by accident either. Think of a way you can teach your child about their input, output, and impact upon the interlacing web of life in which we exist.
- Start with a backyard or lasagna garden (a no-dig organic composting garden). Teach your children how to grow the producers in the food chain. If a garden seems like too much of a stretch, start with germinating a couple of kidney beans in a glass jar or taking care of a small potted herb you buy from the grocery store.
- Research shows that the more children can be involved in growing the food they eat, the more willing and interested they are in trying those new foods or increasing their consumption of healthy vegetables and fruits.
- Try your hand at catch-and-release fishing. Once they've learned to fish, give them the mission of bringing home dinner. They'll be excited by the challenge and eager to try their catch. Teach them how to clean the fish

and cook it in a healthy way. When the day comes that they eat something they kill, a whole new value of life is learned. They'll be ready for the next trip to the pond by the time their plates are clean.

- While you're eating together as a family, capture teachable moments at the dinner table. Start a discussion around the benefits your children's bodies are receiving by eating the fish and vegetables on their plates. What organism did the fish eat to grow and survive? What plant or smaller organism did its prey eat? What environments are necessary for all of those organisms in the food chain to not only survive but to thrive? How do you and your child affect those environments on a daily basis? Or better yet, what can you and your child do to protect the habitats and environments that are critical for the survival of the organisms of the food chain you're eating for dinner?

- Putting food on the table that you have gathered or grown sure makes you appreciate life and good-tasting, healthy food. It is amazing how many living organisms (plants and animals) are ingested to keep us alive each day!

8

Water Buffalo

communication

IT WAS NOVEMBER and we were making the final preparations for our first ever SwampFest, a one-of-a-kind festival
at Playcard Swamp, which grew to be attended by as many as
seven thousand people. The festival was scattered over eighty
acres of pristine land that included a livestock barn, a huge garden, hay fields, enchanting forests, and the black water of the
Playcard Swamp, teaming with gators and water moccasins (cot-
tonmouth)—certainly not your usual stroll in the park. Believe
it or not, there isn't a better place for a party than in a swamp.

Over the years of teaching hands-on science at Playcard,
I had taken people into the swamp by canoe to help me hang
wood duck boxes, identify plants and trees, do water quality
samples, and just go exploring. From the experiences I already
had under my belt in that swamp, I had a feeling that it was

too dangerous to turn "city slickers" loose without supervision during our upcoming SwampFest. But I realized that I had lost that battle when I saw a member of the board haul in four canoes for the festival participants to use. All I could do was pray for their safety and hope for the best.

As with any large event, the show day starts early. We were there at sunup and soon thereafter the other event volunteers arrived. Local farmers started filing into the barn, bringing their newborn animals for the children to see and touch.

One volunteer was gathering all the supplies for the rocket launch and putting new batteries in the bullhorn so that the kids could hear his instructions for the competition. Other volunteers were drawing out the ring for the turtle race and bullfrog jumping contest in the sandy ground. The oxen were being unloaded and harnessed for their day of pulling a wagon full of laughing children. Some of our Native American friends were spreading their deer hides and hanging the dream catchers over the doorway of the round hut, while others started a fire in the center of the Native American village, preparing to cook a delicious venison stew. Facilitators came from all over to set up their activities for the children of Horry County that day.

The problem was that everyone coming to the festival didn't *know* our swamp and that made for, well, a rather dangerous opportunity of fun and learning.

The morning wasn't too far under way when a volunteer came running up to me saying that a Playcard board member had also ordered a large water buffalo to be delivered, and now the delivery men wanted to know where to unload it.

My first thought was, "Great . . . now you tell me." In preparation for SwampFest's debut, we had been working with

FFA students for the past several *months* building pens to house the influx of turkeys, donkeys, calves, ponies, miniature horses, oxen, guineas, goats, pigs, and so on that were scheduled to attend the party. Even with great pens, new animals on a farm can cause problems. Cocky Locky, our red bantam rooster had almost been killed by a visiting tom turkey just a few days prior to the event, and the blood on my hat proved it!

I told the volunteer that we did not have a pen ready to contain a water buffalo. And running through my mind were images of my recent, too-close-for-comfort experience with another water buffalo. My sister Libby had invited our family to one of those safari experiences outside of Atlanta where you ride in your car through fields of wild animals, taking in the scenery and, at times, getting closer than you'd like to the exhibits. Birney was driving, Tyler and Lauren were in the back seat, and I was soaking in all the exotic animals from the front seat of our station wagon. At first, it was a great experience. Then, the kids started fussing. I turned around to help Lauren, then five years old, get a snack out of the cooler. With my head near the floorboard of the back seat, I didn't see the animals getting closer to the car, and no one bothered to mention it. When I turned back around to face forward, I was about two inches away from the slobbery mouth of a water buffalo. I screamed! Birney started laughing and encouraged me to pet him or at least greet our visitor in a more polite manner. He was absolutely huge, and I was scared to death. That's when seven-year-old Tyler thought he'd be helpful and try to make the water buffalo move back out of the car. He picked up something in the back seat, reached out his window, and slapped the water buffalo on the hindquarters. The mad buffalo started kicking our station wagon in a raging frenzy. I thought it was all over for me. Somehow the water buffalo managed to get his enormous horns back out through my window without killing me in the process. I had never been so happy to drive away—alive—in all my life.

That was it for me. I already wanted nothing else to do with water buffaloes, and now they were unloading one for our first SwampFest. I gave strict orders to the volunteer to not let them unload it until I had a chance to talk with James Blanton, the owner of the barn. The volunteer could hear the fearful intensity in my voice and knew I was serious.

After looking all over and then calling his wife, I finally tracked Mr. Blanton down. He was at the doctor's office.

"M'am, this is an emergency," I pleaded with the receptionist. "Please let me talk with Mr. Blanton." She also could hear my intense cry for help, and after a few seconds on hold, Mr. Blanton came to the phone. He agreed that they had to wait until he got there so that he could build a sturdy pen before they unloaded the water buffalo. In the meantime the men who brought the water buffalo kept sending the festival volunteer to ask me for an answer to their question—"what is the hold up?" I refused to go out and talk with them; my nerves were already shot with the thought of having that thing at our first event. I decided that Mr. Blanton could be the one to handle the buffalo when he arrived, not me.

Mr. Blanton arrived about forty-five minutes later with materials from his hardware store heavy enough for a pen. He had been rushing around so much, building the contraption as fast as possible, that he was about out of breath when he said, "Where is the water buffalo? The pen is built. Let's go unload him."

We followed the volunteer over to where the buffalo was waiting to be unloaded. I walked behind Mr. Blanton, taking precaution this time to keep my body as far away from the buffalo's horns as possible. As we got closer, the volunteer introduced us to four men in National Guard military uniforms who were, I'm sure at this point, tired of waiting. The water buffalo they had brought turned out to be a water tank for festival visitors to use for drinking purposes. There was no two-thousand-pound beast to be found. Needless to say, I was embarrassed. Mr. Blanton could not stop laughing. He had just run out of a doctor's exam for the placement of a water tank!

Whenever people in Horry County wanted to introduce me with a good laugh, they always had a way of remembering this story. For me, the start of our SwampFest adventures began with a lesson well learned—the art of communication is well worth developing.

 TAKE A MINUTE TO MUSE . . .

Good communication makes life a whole lot easier. Learning to listen, understand, articulate your thoughts clearly, and assure comprehension by your listener is often easier said than done. Certainly, it is a skill to pass on to our children as young as possible.

Many of our communication errors stem from not taking the time to be sure what we heard was actually what the communicator was intending to say. If only I had taken the time to understand before I jumped to conclusions—a water tank and a water buffalo are two entirely different scenarios! ("Water buffalo" is the military term for a water tank.)

The same can be true with our spouse and children. Many family conflicts can be avoided by taking the time to truly hear and understand what our spouse and children are saying or *meaning to say* through their words.

Think about your recent conversations with your spouse and children.

- What are some of the moments when you knew you hit the bull's-eye with your communication—your children felt heard, understood, valued, and loved?
- What components of your communication made those experiences so successful?
- How might you apply those components to the current conversations you're having?
- Have you hit any communication glitches recently?
- Are there any communication "messes" you need to clean up between yourself and your children? Teaching them not only how to communicate well but also how to restore the relationship when a communication error occurs is just as valuable.

Remember, the goal of communication within a family is not to agree; it is to understand. So often we fight to convince each other to see life exactly the way we do that we fail to honor the perspective the other person has—especially a child's perspective—thereby belittling the other person's feelings, opinion, and viewpoint.

- Instead, how can you show your spouse or children that your love is bigger than having to agree on everything you discuss?

- How will you focus your priority on understanding each other and making sure each member of your family *feels understood* this week?
- How will honoring your child's perspective and seeking to understand her viewpoint build her self-confidence and self-worth, even when you don't agree?

CREATE YOUR OWN FOREVER WILD EXPERIENCE . . .

(Appropriate for toddlers and up)

Can you think of an animal that can communicate without using its mouth? It rubs its wings together very fast and creates high sounding chirps. You guessed it—a cricket!

Here's a fun game you can play with your children. First, divide into two teams, one parent and child paired up together against the other parent-child pair. Next, decide how you will each communicate to each other without using your mouths: hitting sticks or rocks together, clapping your hands—you get the idea. The parent will be blindfolded and, using your chosen method of communication, both of you will "call" back and forth to each other until the parent successfully finds the child. The game begins with both parent and child leaving the place where they were and going to a location where they can't see each other. Blindfolded parents, begin "calling" your babies!

(Appropriate for middle school and up)

Here's another fun adventure that's great for an outdoor birthday party or with some other group of people. If you've never been turkey hunting, you don't know what fun you're missing! Turkey hunters have the best camouflage equipment and face paint of them all. And you can experience the fun without actually going hunting. Pick up a few turkey callers from your local outdoor store, or go to www.nwtf.org (National Wildlife Turkey Federation) for great resources. Before you start, get familiar with the turkey calls and learn to mimic the sound of the wild birds. Once you sound like a turkey, you're ready to play.

First, choose one child or parent to dress up in camouflage and hide in the woods—playing the role of the tom turkey. Next choose one other parent or child dressed in camouflage to hide in the woods and play the role of the hen. Give the turkey callers to the "tom" and the "hen." While they go hide in the woods, the rest of the people should close their eyes and listen to nature's sounds. Give the turkeys about ten minutes or enough time to hide. Then the "tom" and the "hen" will call back and forth four times, while the group of people searches through the woods trying to find them. If the group can't find them before the fourth call, the turkeys win the game.

9

Milking the Snake
what you'll do for your kids

I GOT A CALL from Michael. "Twig, Kim and I are out of town for a couple of weeks. Can you feed my snake for me while we're gone?"

"Sure," I replied. "What do you usually feed Ringo?"

"Toads."

"How often?"

"Oh, just throw three or four toads in the aquarium with him. There should be enough water in there to last. One feeding of toads will hold the snake until we get back. I really appreciate it," Michael concluded.

As usual, we had a backyard full of children. I called them together and asked if anyone wanted to go with me to feed Michael's garter snake, Ringo. Tyler and Lauren excitedly said yes and their buddies joined in. "How do you feed a snake?" Lauren asked.

"Well," I said, "first we have to catch some snake food."

"How do we do that?" asked Tyler.

"First we'll cut on all of our outdoor lights. The lights will attract insects, and then the frogs and toads will come to eat the insects. So are any of you brave enough to catch a toad?" I asked, hoping I'd have some takers. After they all looked at each other, the boys piped in first and then the girls mustered up the courage. I finally heard a few *I am*'s!

We lived in a neighborhood where all the children happened to be about the same age, young elementary school kiddos with curious and adventurous little minds that would be willing to try anything if it sounded halfway fun. I figured now was the perfect time to teach them about frogs and toads, and how to make a frog house. Every child should experience that joy, right?

"Okay, the first thing we need to do if we're going to catch a frog is to make a home to put him in when we catch him. We can put the toads in this box to take them to the snake," I said, holding up an old shoebox, "but we'll make a nice home for our frogs here in the yard because we're not going to feed them to the snake."

"Mom, how do you make a froggie house?" asked Lauren.

"All right, come over here," I said, taking them near the spigot in the backyard and a pile of dirt we had just hauled in for the flower beds. "Let's do this together. Everybody mix some water with several handfuls of dirt and make a big mud pie, but don't get it too wet or it won't work. Now, let's take off our shoes." The children laughed and giggled, so excited to feel the mud between their fingers and bare toes. "Now, cover up one of your feet with your mud pie. This is the very important part: without moving your foot, pat the dirt down over your foot until you can't see your skin anymore. Make sure you leave your ankle and your heel uncovered—that will be the door to your froggie house. Then stand as still as you can and let the dirt dry for a few minutes. When it dries, I want you to slide your foot out, just like you're slowly pulling your foot out of a bedroom slipper, as slowly as possible to keep your froggie house intact."

The next few minutes were hilarious. The kids looked like little flamingos with one leg straight and the other leg cocked as they bent over to artistically form the mud pies on their toes. I worked just as hard trying not to laugh out loud as they compared their globs of mud and tried so hard to balance their little bodies without completely falling over. Lauren screamed, "Mommy, look at my froggie house. Isn't it pretty? I'm putting rocks on mine!"

I smiled and said, "That's perfect, Lauren. You did a great job."

I ran into the garage and grabbed a hopper of old tennis balls while the children were putting the final touches on their froggie homes. "Okay," I said. "Everyone get one of these tennis balls and use it for the door of your home. It's just about dark. Let's go catch some frogs and toads! Remember, toads are brown and have bumps on them. The frogs you'll find are probably going to be green and feel smooth when you touch them."

There sure was a lot of squealing going on as the children ran around the yard peeking under bushes and digging up old leaves. They squealed in excitement when they spotted one, not to mention when they tried to make their little hands close up around a hopping amphibian. They screamed every time the toad or frog moved. Somehow, to my amazement, everyone wound up catching one and enclosing it safely inside a froggie house. After a while, their interests turned from the frogs and toads to wrestling in the grass and playing on the tree swings, so I decided it was time to go feed Ringo. I called all the children together, and we separated the frogs from the toads. The frogs went back into the froggie houses and the toads went into the old shoebox.

"Does anyone want to go with me to feed the snake?" I asked. All their hands darted to the sky in unison. I laughed, still amused by their limitless curiosity. We piled in the station wagon and in a few minutes we were in Kim and Michael's garage observing a hungry, twenty-six-inch-long garter snake. I asked the children a few questions. "How does a snake eat? Does the snake have teeth like we do? Will he swallow his food alive and whole, or bite it in two and chew it up before swallowing it?"

They all got closer to the aquarium and put their noses to the glass. They stared at the snake, trying to see if they could spot any teeth in Ringo's mouth.

"Okay, here we go!" I said, as all eyes turned to me. I picked up the shoebox and dumped its contents into Ringo's glass aquarium. The toads jumped around happily, oblivious to the predator that was watching them. Ringo knew his dinner was near. I wasn't quite sure how the children would respond but figured it would be another good opportunity for them to learn one more lesson of life: the food chain. We all watched, staring at the hopping toads and Ringo's slow, stalking movements. Then it happened. Ringo struck at one of the toads, and the children jumped. The guys oohed and aahed, impressed with the sudden aggressiveness of the kill. Lauren started screaming,

"Mom, Ringo ate the toad! That's my toad! Make him spit it out, Mom! That snake can't eat my toad!"

That's when I realized that my little five-year-old might not be quite ready for the food chain lesson. She was still in love with every animal she touched and somehow saw herself as the surrogate mother of all animals—even amphibians.

Right about then Tyler hollered, "But Lauren, the snake has swallowed him whole. *The snake has already eaten your toad!*"

"Make him spit him out, Momma," Lauren kept demanding, as the tears welled up in her eyes. Her little heart just couldn't take it.

What drama! How in the world did I turn a simple feeding demo into an impossible toad rescue? Retrieving a swallowed toad was beyond my experience, but I knew I had to try to do something. I grabbed the snake, held him upside down and started milking the snake by pushing the toad back toward the snake's mouth. Finally, the toad fell out of Ringo's mouth, covered in thick, mucous saliva.

Lauren ran over, gently picked up her toad, wiped him off on her tee shirt, and sighed. "He's all right, Mom. He's just sweating."

🕐 TAKE A MINUTE TO MUSE . . .

- Childhood is more fun with lots of neighborhood kids. The rule to "stay outside in each other's yards" is not only a safety rule; it is actually the key ingredient to the recipe of how to have the most self-entertaining, creative adventures possible as a kid. Just make sure your children know who has a parent or caregiver at home so they can get help quickly when they need it. Eventually, they'll need it.

- A kindergartener (or younger child) might not truly understand that "catching toads to go feed the snake" actually means "catch a toad that you will then give to a snake and watch it be eaten . . . alive . . . and whole!"

The reality is a mom (or dad) will do ANYTHING to try to fix one of her unintentional mistakes—including milking a snake. Think about a time when your parent went to extreme measures to keep you from emotional harm, intentionally "cleaned up the mess" of something they didn't realize would hurt you, or helped you fix a problem that seemed hopeless.

- How did you experience their love in that moment?
- How has that moment affected the rest of your life?

There are times when you do have to do everything within your power as a parent to support and lead your children forward. In many instances, there's often just one moment to respond, and then it is too late. Life demands decisive action or you'll end up with the passive outcome you never wanted in the first place.

As parents, even when we fail to act in that moment or when our acting is a moment too late, we can restore the emotional trust and heal the wounds of our children by taking the time to talk through the situation with them. Be intentional about going back and recapping the whole experience with your child. Listen to how they see and understand what happened and take decisive action to bring truth into their experience. Lies breed in places of darkness. Your love can shine the light on their misunderstanding. Even if you can't "fix" the situation to be "as good as new," you can communicate your heart's desire towards them and restore your connection with each other.

Some of the biggest obstacles that hinder us in our adult years originate from a misunderstanding, an incorrectly interpreted situation, or an unresolved wound from our childhood. Those wounds, perspectives, and beliefs affect the way we see ourselves, understand our world, and conduct our lives as adults. They are powerful. Being intentional to bring truth to your child's understanding of the situation now (how they are internalizing the situation, how the situation alters their view of the people involved, how the situation impacts what they believe about their place in this world, etc.) is much more valuable than inadvertently letting them believe the lie all their life.

☀ CREATE YOUR OWN FOREVER WILD EXPERIENCE . . .

More and more families in America live far away from each other, so planning special times where all the children gather is a treasure they'll never forget. What if you decided to host all your grandchildren or nieces and nephews at your home for their first cousins' camp? When was the last time they all got together for an extended period of time with the sole purpose of connecting, getting to know each other, and having fun? Even as adults, they will look back on their cousins' camp experiences as some of the most memorable times. You never know, you might just start a family tradition that they will continue with their children's cousins too. If you don't have an extended family, you can give your kids the "cousin" experience by doing the same thing with family friends.

The key to cousins' camp is creating unstructured play times for the children to create their own fun. Instead of furnishing a list of activities for you to do with them, here are a few ideas to help you create the environment for them to learn to play together—on their own. These are just a few ideas to prime the pump of your creativity. I'm sure you have many great ideas in mind already!

- Provide a tent for your kids to pitch in your backyard. Let all the children brave the night outside.
- Instruct them that they can come inside today only to use the bathroom and eat; today is going to be a day outside.
- Unplug all phones, radios, TVs, computers, and electronic games for the week—encourage them to think outside the box and figure out a new way to play.
- Interlace their unstructured play times with really special activities that you do as a big family with the grandparents, parents, and children together. Think of activities that you wouldn't normally do in your busy day-to-day life. Perhaps a big game of kickball in the yard—adults against kids—or running a homemade obstacle course through the forest, seeing which family will take home the braggin' rights.

It is through unstructured play that our children develop the social and interpersonal skills they need to thrive in today's world. They learn to problem solve when they don't have an adult to give them the answers. They learn how to settle their own disputes, even if it comes to blows, and eventually see the value in getting along. They learn to be resourceful and think creatively. They learn how to appreciate the simple pleasures of life and enjoy serenity. Most importantly, they learn that they are the only one responsible for making themselves happy. It's not entertainment that makes us happy; it's a conscious decision to find a way to be content.

As adults, we're expected to work and play together with other people. If we furnish a list of activities for our children and constantly make it our aim to entertain them, we impede the creativity that childhood is begging to teach them.

10

Ghost Cat
making tracks

"THIS IS NO PLACE for a lady," stammered an old-timer entering the front door of the Center.

"It sho' ain't," added his friend. "We come here to warn you."

I could tell from their worn work boots and tanned tobacco-barn smelling skin that these fellas were from around here. They definitely had my attention.

I invited the men to come in and sit down. Our donor, James Blanton, had taken me around and introduced me to our neighbors when I had first started, but I had not met these two men in the neighborhood gatherings.

For weeks, I had been marking and mapping trails through the swamp at Playcard Environmental Education Center. We had started with a gift of eighty acres, but grew to be able to teach off of some of Mr. Blanton's farmland and ponds.

"People been huntin' this swamp for years and if somebody calls the law on them, the law knows they can just get buried and never be heard of again." There was a long silence.

"What you goin' do when you run into the ghost cat?" the larger man said, waiting for my answer.

"What is a ghost cat?" I hesitantly asked.

They laughed saying, "You *are* a lady, just like you look. Don't know nothin' 'bout the outdoors, just book learnin'."

They now had me angry, but I needed to learn about our swamps, so I tried to control my words.

"Well, sir, yesterday," I confidently began, "I got a call from a man who had just moved his family into a trailer in another swamp about eight miles from here. He said that he heard a lion roaring in the woods right outside his door the night before last. So I asked him if he'd seen the big cat. He said no, but was certain there were two of them and that the female must have been in heat by the way she was screaming. He got completely exasperated with me on the phone and said, 'Look lady, I came from the city where we have zoos. I know a lion when I hear one. My question to you is what kind of wild—not penned up—lion lives around here, and what can I do about it?'"

I leaned in closer with a stern face and asked the old-timers, "Is *this* your ghost cat?"

They laughed, "Could be, if he is solid black and BIG!"

"Okay then, I need you to help me," I said. "I *am* a lady—thank you for your compliment," I continued. "My loving husband sends me to work out here each day with a loaded shotgun. He does not want to raise our five-year-old daughter and seven-year-old son without their mother. But I need your help to find this ghost cat."

They leaned forward, eager to hear just what I had in mind.

"My parents raised me on the Savannah River in the winter and the May River in the summer, and through the years, Dad made a pretty good tracker out of me. If we can prove there are endangered species like the ghost cat—we actually call him the black panther in the Savannah River Swamp—then we can get federal money to help us preserve a wetlands corridor that would flow from here at our Playcard Swamp all the way into Winyah Bay." Their eyes got big when they realized just how much land that covered: all of Playcard Swamp, as well as the Pleasant Meadow Swamp, and the wetlands around the Little and the Big Pee Dee Rivers—all the way from up here near the North Carolina border to Winyah Bay.

"So, if you would be so kind, gentlemen, could you give me a call when you find a good track? When you do, please cover it. I'll come over immediately and make a positive and negative cast—that will be the proof we need." They looked at each other and back at me; they were up for the challenge.

"I'll be looking for his track too, and we'll see who finds the ghost cat first. Remember, his track is unique; pay attention to the way his toes curve and the shape and position of the pad. You might find it helpful to look up information on the Eastern Cougar."

"Yes'm," they said, as they shook my hand and nestled their dusty leather hats back on their heads. I gripped the first one's hand, looked him in the eye and said, "You know, this cat is pretty close to extinction. You would be doing something really important by helping us save this land and keep these last few wild places like Playcard Swamp from being developed."

They looked at me, tipped their hats, and walked out the door—this time a little more confident in the five-foot-three-inch little lady they had come to warn. The word spread, and many people came to work with us at the Center—learning about land trusts, conservation easements, and the role of education in preserving wilderness places.

A few months later, after the ghost cat warning from the neighbors and still no sign of the critter, I received a call from Dr. Harvey, one of our friends who lived on the Waccamaw River. He had been out that morning at sunrise, walking with his dogs on their property, and the dogs jumped a deer. The deer had run straight into an electrical fence and died immediately of a heart attack. Dr. Harvey called to see if there was any way I could come get the deer and use it. The deer was in great physical shape and could still be eaten if I could get to it soon.

It was winter, and Eustace Conway from Turtle Island Preserve was scheduled to teach workshops for two classes of middle school students at the Center that morning. My dad raised me by the hunter's code: if you kill it, be ready to eat it. The teachers thought this would be a great hands-on learning experience for their students. After talking with Eustace, we called a game warden and he brought the deer out to the Center for us.

Eustace dressed out the deer in the traditional Native American way and gave the students a deeper understanding of the value of one animal's life. He even brain tanned the hide and made glue out of the hooves. No part of the deer was wasted. After the students had gone back to their school, I finally persuaded Eustace to give me the deer's digestive system.

I wanted to see if I could bait up an area to attract the cougar. We had just plowed large fire breaks with a twelve-row tractor around one of the fields near the far end of the swamp property. I knew that's where I wanted to go. Deer often came to graze on the grain fields we farmed. The firebreaks around the fields were the perfect places to read tracks.

I emptied the buckets of guts at the edge of a fire break and walked away, hoping for the best. I could hardly sleep that night, excited that I was possibly only one day away from finally spotting the ghost cat. I got to work early the next morning, just after daybreak and went straight to the field. As I neared the firebreak, I saw the tracks of the herd walking together down the side of the field. Then the tracks started scattering, going in all directions. And there it was—a clean, undeniable cougar track in the freshly plowed dirt near where I had dumped the deer remains yesterday. Cheering with excitement inside, I covered the track until I could come back with plaster of Paris to make a few casts. Scavengers had already recycled most of the deer guts.

I started walking away, but after a few feet, the curiosity about the deer scattering pattern got the best of me. I turned around and started following some of the deer tracks again. One deer seemed to be jumping and running erratically in and out and down the plowed area. I walked quite a distance just looking to see if I could piece the story together. That's when I saw an unusual pile of sticks next to the woods, up ahead on one side of the firebreak. We had always cleared that area for fire safety. When I got closer, I could see there was a deer under the brush. I had never seen an animal cover its dead prey. Even more curious now, I removed some of the branches and dug deeper until I found the proof I needed—fresh blood in the neck area. The cougar had jumped the deer. In a panic, the deer kept running and then jumped, trying anything to get the cougar off his back. But the cougar succeeded in bleeding him with his claws. He may have even severed his spinal cord with his bite.

Then it hit me that the cougar could be close by, watching me uncover his kill! The more I thought about it, the more frightened I became. I ran all the way back to the Center, arriving just a few minutes before a bus load of students got there.

As soon as I finished teaching late that afternoon, I got my shotgun and called my two neighbor friends to come back with me to the firebreaks. Of course when we got there the covered deer was gone, but we were able to make a few good casts of the cougar tracks. We finally had the proof we needed that Playcard was a habitat for the big, mysterious ghost cat.

I continued to track the cougar for three and a half years at Playcard without seeing him. The cougar was so elusive, but the signs of its presence were undeniable. The tracks were enormous.

About three years after I got the cougar tracks, I had to go to the Washington, D.C., area for four days to help facilitate a wetlands conference. (By the way, we never did get a federal grant to protect the proposed wetlands corridor, but citizens in our community continued to help us save additional wetlands.) It was a tough time to leave the farm at Playcard because many of our animals were giving birth to their young. The goal was to always keep a few babies in the barnyard for teaching purposes, and we had about every kind of farm animal you could imagine.

As customary for barnyard animals, many of the mothers would leave the big barn when it was time to deliver. The mother would hide her newborn baby or babies in the woods, telling them not to move and not to make a sound until she returned. She was going to the barn to eat and drink. And instinctively, the babies knew to stay put and quiet. In another two days she would bring the babies back up to the barn and they would join all the other animals, sleeping and eating together. That's why, when I heard the newborn cry of a lamb, I became alarmed.

I was trying to pack up and leave for the conference the next afternoon, so I didn't have much time. I jumped on the golf cart and headed for the barn. It sounded like the cry was coming from the upper pasture beyond the pond. In a rush, I got out of the golf cart and started hiking toward the sound of the cry. The upper pasture was a little ways from the end of the trail and I needed to cross over a few fences, so the rest of the journey would be on foot through the woods. Pushing my way through branches, I stepped on a fallen limb and it cracked loudly into two pieces.

The next thing I knew, a cougar was running straight for me. I tried to run, but that lion was so big and I was so scared, I just collapsed. I felt weak all over. The cougar jumped. I thought that was it for me.

He must have sailed twenty to thirty feet in the air before he touched the ground again. I lay there watching to see what would happen next, as I prayed. "Thank you, Lord; he is still running and I am alive! What a joke! I used to think I wanted to finally see the cougar that I have been tracking and studying for so long."

The lamb was still bleating, and it sounded more distressed than before. My knees were so weak from the close call with the big cat that I wasn't sure I could stand, but I knew I couldn't lie there any longer and listen to the lamb cry. So I pulled myself up and started hiking toward the sound again. I could hardly hear his faint bleating by the time I got to him. The lamb was hemorrhaging pretty badly in the head area. I wrapped him in my shirt and ran as fast as I could back to the car to get to the vet's office before it was too late.

With blood all over my clothes, and a faint newborn lamb in my hands, I desperately asked, "Can you help me?"

He looked at me with compassion and said, "Well now, let's have a good look at the little guy." Dr. Smith quickly ran his hands over the lamb, assessing the damage.

"Do you know what caused this wound?" I asked.

"It looks like a cut and not a puncture wound," he said, staring at it closely, "Was there any metal around the pasture where you found the lamb?"

His question reminded me. "Well, I did see a piece of tin roofing that had blown off of the tobacco barn." Somehow, I was relieved the cougar hadn't gotten ahold of the lamb. As he continued to quickly work on the lamb, I told Dr. Smith about my face-to-face encounter with the ghost cat.

"Maybe," Dr. Smith continued, "the crying of the lamb attracted the cougar. He was probably near the lamb and ready for the kill when you stepped on the branch and spooked him."

I picked up the lamb again. It had stopped crying. Dr. Smith said, "Leave it here with me, Twig. He's dead. You did all you could for him. You need to go home and take care of yourself. You've had a close call."

I wanted to cry. It seemed so unfair for the lamb to die now—especially after everything I went through to get to him. "Thanks, Dr. Smith, I think I will," I whispered as I put the lamb down and headed for the door.

I was shutting the door behind me when Dr. Smith blurted out, "Twig, one more thing—just how big was that cougar anyway?"

Exhausted from the mere thought of all the adrenaline that had pumped through my body less than an hour before, and weary from the loss of holding the little lamb as it took its last breath, I looked back at him and said, "Big. He had a very long, black-tipped tail. But not counting the length of his tail, his body seemed to be seven or eight feet long. What I saw of his underside was lighter in color, but he was similar to a deer's color, not black. He was enormous!"

(L) TAKE A MINUTE TO MUSE . . .

Just like animals, we humans leave tracks that identify who we are and what kind of impact we leave on the world as we live our life. Think about the "tracks" your parents left behind. Think about the "tracks" you're leaving behind. What do your tracks say about your character, your mission in life, and your contribution to the world?

- What can you do this week to teach your child about the "tracks" they are leaving behind?
- What is a meaningful, rewarding way you can leave your tracks on your neighborhood, another family, or the people you meet this week?
- Just as you would make a plaster of Paris track of an animal footprint, after you and your child have participated in a meaningful, impactful experience together, take the time to "make a track" of your experience in your own creative way, so that they see the real impact of their steps.
- And just as you would make a game out of tracking animals, make a game out of making our world a better

place. When you do this with young children and they return to that place later on, the first thing they want to do is to run and see if their "track" is still recognizable.

- What are some meaningful, practical ways you can expose your children to people who might not have a warm bed to sleep in tonight, a delicious meal to eat, or a loving family to come home to? How can you teach your children to be generous with their love, riches, and skills? How can you challenge your children to help make our world a better place with the resources and skills they have right now?

CREATE YOUR OWN FOREVER WILD EXPERIENCE . . .

Have you ever tracked an animal with your children and made a cast of the footprint together? If not, there are lots of good books to teach you how—it's a very simple and economical process. Not only is it a fun way to keep a dated record of your exploratory findings but it's an easy way to show others just how big your critter really was! Make a game or challenge with your children. See who can identify the animal first or collect the greatest variety of tracks in a year.

Take advantage of the tracking experience to teach important life concepts to your child. For example, ask questions to help your little one understand and value the environment and role of that animal in our ecosystem.

- Where is the water source that makes this a good habitat for this animal?

- Is this animal an herbivore? If so, which plants do you see that it eats?
- Is this animal a carnivore? What kinds of animals would it eat? If it didn't kill and eat those animals, what would happen to our animal friend that we're tracking?
- Is this animal an omnivore? What are the features of its body that help it eat both plants and animals?
- Where do you think this animal sleeps? Is it more active at night or during the day? Why?
- What can we know about this animal by looking at its footprint?

Or maybe tracking plants is more your speed. Keep track of the changes a tree undergoes in the course of a year, keep track of the different types of trees and shrubs in your yard or your neighborhood, or keep track of the sizes of various trees.

- Take a photo of the same tree on the same date each month and have your child compare the photos. Talk about what the tree needs to survive and how it gets those elements. Think about what animals make their homes in the tree, and what else the tree provides to its environment.
- Sketch or take a photo of two or three different plants or trees in your area. Learn their names and see if your child can spot that same variety as you travel around town. Do a few more next month.
- Measure the tree trunks and estimate the heights of different varieties of trees in your neighborhood. If you really fall in love with this activity, you can progress all the way into the competitive world of big tree hunting.

11

Arnold
a pig with personality

A KINDERGARTEN TEACHER can only contain a piglet in a classroom for just so many days before the noises and odors start to give her secret away. That's when I got a call to come pick up the pig.

Arnold was a cute little fellow. He was only about eight pounds, black and white all over, and was up to date on all of his shots. The children had just finished their unit on *Charlotte's Web* and had, by now, completely fallen in love with Arnold. Even though they claimed he was house broken, the teacher knew he just couldn't grow up in the classroom. Besides, she had recently received another reminder from her principal that the pig had to go.

As the director of Playcard Environmental Education Center, a "classroom without walls" as I fondly regarded it, I still had to get permission to teach with the piglet. Chances were, since we had a working farm and the capacity to handle a little piglet, it wouldn't be a problem. Even so, I made the call to the district office to see if I could have a few minutes of the superintendent's time that afternoon.

After all the appointments were set, I dashed over to Tyler's school to pick up our first grade son a little early, so that I could make it to Socastee Elementary and the district office before everyone left for the day. Tyler knew there was something fun coming when he saw the cardboard box lined with newspapers in the back seat; to him, that normally meant we were about to transport a critter of some sort.

Tyler's job was to keep Arnold in the box—not the easiest task on a thirty-mile trip. When Arnold squealed, Tyler screamed. Arnold would knock the box top open and Tyler would push down with all his might to try to keep the top on. It was the best wrestling match Tyler had ever picked, and Arnold was winning! Arnold started running circles in the box trying to get out, and Tyler held on tight while he was knocked around the back seat. Oinks, grunts, laughs, screams, squeals, bumps, and bounces bellowed from the back seat of our station wagon. I was driving as fast as I could to get us to the district office.

Thankful that we had finally arrived and my son didn't have a black eye yet, I quickly unloaded the pig and brushed Tyler's hair down with my fingers. "Tuck your shirt in Tyler," I said, hoping my nose hadn't grown too accustomed to the smell of the pig to tell whether my little boy still smelled like a human.

"Okay, here's the plan," I said, squatting down to Tyler's eye level, "I just need to go in there and have a very quick conversation with the superintendent. You did a great job keeping the piglet in the back seat when we were driving. Hold out your hands. I want you to give Arnold a big bear hug like your daddy gives you in the morning. Hold him tight in your arms. I need you to wait very quietly outside of the superintendent's office while I'm in there, in case he needs to see Arnold. I'll be right out." Tyler nodded his head in agreement and whispered, "Yes, Mommy. I can't wait to give Arnold a bear hug!" I wasn't about to leave our son or the piglet in the hot car, so this was our only option. Arnold calmly went into Tyler's arms and seemed relieved to be out of that box.

We walked inside. All the doors were closed to the offices, and no one was in the hallway. "Perfect," I thought as we scurried down the cold tile floor. It seemed to echo with every step. I positioned Tyler by the office door, and went in for the meeting. Just as I got the question out of my mouth, "Would it be okay if we bring a little piglet to the Center to teach with on the farm?" squeals and screams erupted from the hallway.

Tyler had decided to put the piglet down to get a drink from the water fountain. And now all the office doors swung open to see a seven-year-old sprawled out on his belly with his arms stretched forward, grabbing a squealing piglet by one hind leg. I couldn't tell who was screaming more, Tyler or the pig.

Permission was granted immediately, just as long as I got that squealing pig out of the administrative building at once! I ran over to Tyler and picked both him and Arnold up in my arms. They looked at each other like two children who had just gotten into a fight—pouty lips and defiant faces—determined to wrestle again. Now all I had to do was make it home with everyone in one piece.

We had a fenced-in backyard at our house to keep the pig in for the night. As soon as we got home, five-year-old Lauren excitedly joined Tyler in putting Arnold out in the yard. Within seconds Arnold became a bulldozer. He had been in a classroom for weeks, but as soon as his feet hit the dirt, he started rooting with his nose.

The children and I stood there in silent amazement. Even though he had never been on soil before, somehow he knew exactly what he was designed to do. Within minutes Arnold's appearance changed. You couldn't spot an inch of white hair on his body. He was slinging black dirt in the air and making an oinking sound that clearly communicated pure joy. The children got down on all fours beside Arnold, and laughed and laughed as he aggressively plowed up the dirt under their fingers and toes.

Right after we got Arnold in the fenced-in backyard, Birney came home. He had already picked up the babysitter on his way home from work and was expecting me to be ready for a romantic Valentine's dinner date for two in Myrtle Beach. I had forgotten about the Valentine's celebration! And to make matters worse, I smelled like a pig!

By the time I showered and dressed, we had missed our reservations. But Birney came up with a wonderful Plan B and we made it out the door for our date after all. We had a good time laughing over dinner about the wild escapades of the day, recounting the thirty-mile wrestling match in the back seat of the car, the quiet, graceful announcement at the district office, and the mud discovery in the back yard. Dinner was always an eventful time of storytelling, but it was especially good that night. More than anything, I was looking forward to our cozy, warm bed and a good night's sleep.

On the way home, Birney suggested that I put Arnold in the dog carrier in the garage for the night. The rate he was going, Arnold would probably find a way out of the backyard by morning. We got in from our date around 11:00 p.m. The children were enjoying their well-deserved rest and the babysitter had even straightened the house. With the house being so calm, I flipped on the outside floodlight and curiously peeked out the back door to make sure we still had a piglet.

To my horror, the backyard looked like a gigantic black mud puddle. I gasped out loud and exclaimed, "How could one little piglet root up all of our grass?"

Birney had just left to take the babysitter home. Stunned and utterly exhausted, I stood there with my head on the storm door, trying to muster up one more ounce of energy to face another stunt our little piglet friend had accomplished in this very long day. After the realization came back to me—that *all* of our grass had been ripped up in the back yard—and the subsequent surge of annoyance ran through my blood, I went in and changed my clothes.

"Surely Arnold will be tired after excavating our entire back yard," I thought as I laced up an old pair of work boots.

That was the first and the last time I have ever tried to catch a pig in a large open area. For the next hour, I ran all over the yard! I got tired of diving in the mud and thought maybe a broom would help me hem him up. That was another mistake! Now he was squealing. All the lights in our neighborhood started coming on. Somehow in my determination to get the pig in the dog carrier, I had forgotten that it was at least 11:30 p.m. at this point, and to make matters worse, we weren't supposed to have pigs in our subdivision! To top it off, the children were now awake.

Birney had gotten home and was enjoying the fiasco with the children from the dining room windows. I was exhausted and completely covered in mud. After an hour of failure, I declared Arnold the winner and decided that I would just have to deal with this in the morning.

Birney got the children back to bed and I headed for the shower, dripping mud down the hallway as I walked. I was just about to get in the shower when something caught my eye out the bathroom window. I put my glasses back on and looked out to see my husband walk right up to Arnold, pick him up by his hind legs, and carry him straight to the garage. Arnold never uttered a sound! I couldn't believe my eyes or my ears! I was speechless and humbled but relieved I wouldn't have to chase that pig in the morning. All I could think about was how in the world did Birney catch that pig without it squealing! It was too late to even care. We all had to go to sleep; 6:00 a.m. was only a few hours away.

The sun rose mighty early the next morning as we sat down for breakfast. I couldn't wait any longer to hear Birney's explanation of his pig-whispering skills. Right as he came into the dining room I erupted in amazement, "Thank you so much, Honey, for catching Arnold last night and putting him in the carrier for me! How in the world did you catch him? And why on earth didn't he squeal when you picked him up?"

Birney had everybody's attention as he began, "Well, when I was a little boy we raised pigs on our farm. When you raise pigs, you eventually learn how to handle them. One of the things I learned was if you hold a pig upside down, it is impossible for him to squeal. And although the broom extended your reach, Twig, you were scaring Arnold the way you were trying to catch him. I decided we had awakened enough neighbors for one night."

Funny thing was, about five minutes later, after we had cleaned up the dishes, grabbed the kids' backpacks, and all headed out the door for the school day, I was greeted by one of those neighbors. Lorie Harmon was standing patiently at her mailbox, just waiting for the mass exit. She hollered, "Twiggy! What in tarnation made those squealing noises from your backyard last night?" Embarrassed, humored, and in a rush to get to school, I laughed out loud, pulled Arnold out of the dog carrier, and introduced him to Lorie. "Lorie, meet Arnold. He had the unfortunate experience of being chased by a broom last night." She just stood there in silence with her jaw dropped, shook her head, and graciously offered to look the other way one more time. It wasn't the first and probably wouldn't be the last time our kind neighbors heard a wild noise from our backyard.

⏱ TAKE A MINUTE TO MUSE . . .

Family life is a circus sometimes, but somehow, no matter how crazy it gets, we sure are thankful to be a part of the show. Learning to roll with the punches and laugh when you feel like crying are two important skills to develop in your parenting journey.

- Can you think of a family adventure that is only humorous *now*, as you look back on it—maybe one of those stunts you played on your parents or a trapeze act one of your children recently tried?

- What is a way you can chronicle the life lessons you've learned through each circus act your family has masterfully performed?
- A recorded chronicle of your parenting experiences, memories, and wisdom not only provides a valuable gift for your children one day when they call home to say, "We're pregnant" but will be a priceless treasure of rich heritage they can share and cherish for years to come. Just as every child loves to climb up on the bed and spend hours staring at pictures of you and your spouse when you were first married or what they looked like when they were infants, the family stories you tell create a rich self-concept. Through your stories, they begin to get a sense of who they are and where they come from. The connection with their heritage provides an anchoring foundation for the developing years ahead.

CREATE YOUR OWN FOREVER WILD EXPERIENCE . . .

There is great value in letting your child share the responsibility of caring for a family pet. If your child has a fish or a spider, I would encourage you to step out on a limb and brave the experience of a pet that they can hold, cuddle, take on walks, groom, and feed daily. If a family pet isn't possible in your situation, perhaps a neighbor would welcome the offer of walking their dog each workday, or maybe your local animal shelter has a program for young volunteers. The life lessons learned through raising or caring for animals are priceless and innumerable. And if you're adventurous, you don't have to limit yourself to the domestic cat or dog: try your hand at a lamb, goat, pig, horse, cow, donkey, or pony. Just remember, they all come with their own personality.

12

Lowcountry Magic
cherishing each moment

CHANGE IS THE UNINVITED GUEST that barges its way into every human life here on earth. Seemingly, the more we try to protect our favorite places and most beautiful memories, the more we realize we are unable to catch the powerful monster and hold it down. Eventually we must come to terms with the impossibility of keeping our life the way it is.

I have watched the storm of change rain down on my beloved hideaway. But when my mind wanders back, I can see the live oak trees draping their massive arms over the road, creating a romantic canopy as you enter the town. A sense of Southern pride wells up inside your throat as you drive past the old cottages flying the South Carolina and American flags from the porches. Next you pass a weathered produce stand with brightly colored fruits and vegetables neatly sorted in handmade baskets. Two black ladies are visiting with each other and enjoying the beautifully gentle day. Their hands are worn yet soft with cocoa oil. Their hair is neatly braided around their heads, and their voices speaking the Geechee-Gullah dialect soothe your ears. You wave, returning their grace of southern manner. The road winds and then finally your eyes behold the beauty of the Lowcountry. The deep hue of the river and the swaying dance of the marsh grass capture your heart and intoxicate you with wonder. Out on the horizon you see a dolphin break water. A majestic white ibis wades in the shallow creek, surveying the area for a quick snack. The wind whispers the name of this sacred place; it carries the sounds of laughter, the scent of an estuary, and the breath of fresh air that you crave whenever you are away from here.

This is the birthplace of my most treasured memories. Each experience is like an epic film in my mind. One in particular makes me laugh just thinking about it. My dad and I had gone out early one morning to beat the hot sun. Going down Bull Creek in the boat, we came up on a pod of dolphins. Several adult bottlenose dolphins were churning up the water and making noises that sounded like laughter. It was dead low tide and the large, shell-free banks of black pluff mud were visible. We drove up closer and could see the noisy game of beach ball they were playing. For the next thirty minutes or so we sat there and watched in utter amazement. First the momma dolphin would swim under the baby and position the baby on her head. Then, in a split second, she would flip the baby into the air. The baby would fly in the air and squeal a couple of times before she hit the soft pluff mud bank and rolled back into the water. Then the next baby and his mother would take their turn until all of them got to play. It was spectacular. You would have thought we were watching Shamu. Bottlenose dolphins have a perpetual smile on their faces, so they always appear to be having fun, but this time you could hear the fun in their squeals.

There are so many memories here like that one. Just being here again makes each moment come alive. In one, my knees are shaking as my ten-year-old body dares to stand up on two water skis. In another, I feel the smooth, thick skin of a dolphin as he artfully balances on the tip of his tail, performing tricks for the audience in our johnboat. I hear the laughter of all the neighborhood kids splashing in the water and running down the beach, racing to dive into the muddy river. I feel the tickling of a fiddler crab as it crawls through my fingers and then burrows in a hole in the sand. I hear the voices of wise men as they sit and talk down at "Old Man's Corner." My dad turns his head and smiles at my sisters and me. The taste of the buttery crab and the hot boiled shrimp fills my mouth. The Marsh Tackies still gallop and wild buffalo still roam free on the islands. I can see the strong men oaring the wooden bateaux toward Daufuskie through the rainbow of sunset colors. I can even feel the excitement of casting my first shrimp net, gigging my first flounder, inching in a crab, conquering the sport of skiing, fighting the hammerhead on the other end of my line, and having pillow fights on the front porch bunk beds.

Yes, this is a special place and even this sanctuary could not be protected from change's whirling path. Now the produce stands have become grocery stores with big parking lots. The sweet spirited ladies walking down the street have become men in ties and briefcases, rushing to work, fighting miles of traffic. Modernized condominiums and rows of houses that look exactly alike have replaced the charming Lowcountry cottages.

The beachfront has been trashed with beer bottles and cigarette butts. The dolphins only dance in the backwaters, fearful of the fast moving props on the loud boats. The chairs at "Old Man's Corner" speak of their abandonment and reveal the sad truth—all men die in this world.

Yet the waves keep moving. They are determined to fight the storm of change, and hold on to the hope that one day my children will have a tiny grain of sand to recreate these experiences. Change cuts grooves in the parts of life that are so dear, yet the May River has held its ground. The river has stayed wild even through the development and passing of time. The constant tides of life, the knock-downs and the get-ups, flow together to create an ocean of experiences each unique to our own name.

Pulling up to the cottage in our station wagon, the children can hardly wait to jump out and race to the water. Birney and I can hardly wait to spend another two weeks making more memories at our hideaway retreat.

🕐 TAKE A MINUTE TO MUSE . . .

Between soccer practice, cooking dinner, doing homework, and making sure the kids have scrubbed behind their ears, the day-to-day life in a family can easily fly by. Before we have time to blink, our newborn is starting kindergarten, our tee-baller is asking for the car keys, and our last one is graduating from college next week. Life happens, fast.

Unfortunately, with the competitive and high-pressure academic and sports environment children are growing up in now, we're losing the time to personally connect with our children. Evening meals are regularly purchased at drive-through restaurants and gulped down in the car on the way to ball practice, piano lessons, or ballet. According to the Nielsen Cross-Platform Report [Q4 2011], the average American watches nearly five hours of video per day (television, computer, gaming, etc.) and most American homes have multiple televisions, in separate rooms of the house. It's very easy to wake your kids up in the morning and not really connect with them again until bedtime.

Just think about it. When was the last time you cooked a meal, turned off the television, and ate around the dinner table as an entire family? When was the last time you stopped *doing* and just spent time *being* together? When was the last time you went for a walk outside as a family or rode bicycles together after dinner instead of turning on the television? How many evenings per week does your child have at home, with unstructured time to explore outside, use her creativity to create her own fun, or even have the chance to make a memory together as a family?

The wonderful news is—you have a choice. You can create a different childhood for your children and a different future for your family.

I challenge you with two action steps. First, write down the vision you have for your family.

- Describe the connection you want to have with each other. Get specific. In what ways will you honor each other, speak to each other, and know each other? What measure of trust, intimacy, peace, and connection will you have in your relationship to each other?
- Vividly describe the memories you want to make together. Think about it from when you're eighty years old and sitting around the dinner table with your grandkids—what

are the stories you want to tell them about their parents' childhood?

- Your ability to step back and see the big picture provides a priceless advantage in the day-to-day rush when it comes to cherishing right now. Seeing, feeling, and tasting the vision you have for your family will empower you to intentionally create the environment now for that vision to root and grow.

Second, the next time you've had another "normal day"—when you're rushing your child out of the house with one sock on and a cleat in the other hand, when you're tapping your finger on the steering wheel hoping the drive-through cashier will stop talking to the driver in front of you and move things along, when you're exhausted from the day and rushing back to start the homework marathon and your child is quietly staring out the car window—ask him. Ask him what he would think about choosing one activity during the week instead of ten. Ask him how he would like to play—would he like to go on a bike ride together instead of watching TV tomorrow evening? Ask him if he wants to build a fort in the woods this weekend instead of going to the amusement park again. Ask him if he would like a simpler life. You might really be surprised.

⌖ CREATE YOUR OWN FOREVER WILD EXPERIENCE . . .

Where is that hideaway retreat for you? Where was it when you were a child? Was it a creek near your home, a forest at the end of the street, or on your grandparent's farm? What were the simple but exciting experiences in nature you had as a child?

Richard Louv in his book *Last Child in the Woods* describes the impact of nature in a child's life most accurately:

> *For children, nature comes in many forms. A newborn calf; a pet that lives and dies; a worn path through the woods; a fort nested in stinging nettles; a damp, mysterious edge of a vacant lot—whatever shape nature takes, it offers each child an older, larger world separate from parents. Unlike television, nature does not steal time; it amplifies it. Nature offers healing for a child living in a destructive family or neighborhood. It serves as a blank slate upon which a child draws and reinterprets the culture's fantasies. Nature inspires creativity in a child by demanding visualization and the full use of the senses. Given a chance, a child will bring the confusion of the world to the woods, wash it in the creek, and turn it over to see what lives on the unseen side of that confusion. Nature can frighten a child, too, and this fright serves a purpose. In nature, a child finds freedom, fantasy, and privacy: a place distant from the adult world, a separate peace.*

Unless you live in the middle of a city, this "create your own forever wild experience" actually requires little input from you for a change; most of the work will come from your children on this one. And in their eyes, to call it work would be a lie. In fact, it's probably one of their most coveted forms of play—free rein to explore the natural world around them. Your part comes in simply recognizing the importance of creating the space in their daily schedule for them go outside and play.

13

Buttercup
the children and the kid

THE PHONE RANG after supper one night. "Twig, our daughter went on a school field trip to Playcard and hasn't stopped talking about all the fun hands-on ways you taught science," he started, as he apologized for calling me so late. "Norah Jane insisted that I call you. One of the nannies on our farm came down with mastitis and died tonight. Her kid is only one day old and won't live if I can't find a family to bottle-feed her and give her a home."

I thought out loud, "Thank you for the offer. I would love to let my own children raise a kid, but we're just not set up for that right now. We live in a subdivision that won't allow goats."

The farmer matter-of-factly said, "Well, the kid will be dead by morning."

There was silence. Then I heard myself say, "Okay, we'll take her." Knowing I hadn't discussed this new addition to our family with anyone, I soon found myself asking directions to his farm. My generous husband lovingly listened as I came back into the living room and explained the crisis situation. With all the kindness and patience one man could ever have, he smiled, somehow knowing that I had already agreed to take the goat.

We bundled the children into the car and left immediately for the farm. It was a dark, cold October night when we were given Buttercup. She was a tiny, tawny-colored briar goat with thin, black-trimmed ears. She had a tuft of white hair on the end of her tail and a soft, flat little nose.

Birney drove us home, and I held the goat in my arms. Tyler, now eight years old, and Lauren, six, sat in the back seat and discussed (as well as two little children can discuss a few hours after their bedtime) until they decided to name her Buttercup.

As soon as we got home, we called Penny, our librarian friend who had a pet goat.

"Penny, I am so sorry to call you this late. We've just been given a baby goat that is really hungry. Her mom died with mastitis, and she hasn't had much milk. I know it's already eleven o'clock, but could you help us keep her alive tonight?"

"Come over and I'll help you," she answered. Relieved at her answer, Birney and I loaded the children and the kid into the car, again.

When we got there, Penny pulled out a few cans of goat's milk from her kitchen cabinet. She diluted some of the milk with a small amount of water, heated it until it was warm, and then poured it into a surgical glove that she had turned inside-out.

She tied the surgical glove shut and then punctured a hole in the end of one of the fingers.

Tyler and Lauren were fascinated with what they saw. "What do you think, Tyler and Lauren?" Penny asked. "Do you think this looks and feels enough like Buttercup's mom's udder that your baby goat will know what to do?" They didn't know what to say. They just watched, wide-eyed. Penny squirted milk into Buttercup's mouth and Buttercup tasted it.

Tyler squealed with laughter and said, "Miss Penny, why is she knockin' that glove with her head? Isn't she supposed to put the finger in her mouth and suck the milk out?"

Penny chuckled and then answered, "That butting is instinctive behavior. Buttercup is butting the glove to make the milk come down, like she would do with her mom's udder and teat."

Before long, Buttercup discovered where the warm milk came from and was sucking the finger like a champ. "Take these milk cans and gloves home with you tonight, and every two hours see if you can get a little more milk into her mouth. She's very weak right now, but I think she'll live," Penny encouraged us.

Birney chuckled as our caravan pulled out of Penny's driveway, "I'll take the first two-hour feeding; you get the wee-hour ones. It'll be just like having an infant again. Won't that be fun?"

I winked at him, and humbly agreed. I was the one who had gotten us into this fiasco in the first place.

The next morning around seven o'clock the grocery store opened and we were finally able to purchase baby bottles and goat's milk. Buttercup was looking stronger already.

She soon became the most social kid ever! When Tyler and Lauren weren't holding her, the other children in the neighborhood were. It was hilarious to watch them dance all around the laundry room floor in their sock feet with both hands on the bottle while Buttercup tried to butt the bottle right out of their fingers. I wasn't sure if more milk ended up on the floor or in Buttercup's mouth, but between the *baaa*s and the squeals of laughter, it seemed like they were all having fun.

I began taking Buttercup to work with me each day at Playcard so we could keep her feedings on some kind of schedule. She was very curious, talked constantly, and never left my side. Her favorite activity was riding in the golf cart or mischievously devising a plan to steal food.

One of her best pranks at Playcard was to wait until all the students were sitting around the outside octagonal picnic tables, then hop up on the bench beside a student and *baaa* in his ear. The student would usually be so surprised that he would jump up from the table and run away, scared to death. In her moment of opportunity, Buttercup would grab his peanut butter and jelly sandwich and try to put the whole thing into her mouth before he came back. I think Buttercup loved PB & J sandwiches more than any other food.

Being the escape artist she was, I wasn't surprised when I got to the Center one Saturday morning and found her out of the pasture with her head hidden in a bunch of nandina, eating the red berries. She would often discover a way to get out and find a few extra goodies to nibble on, but I got really worried this time. When I got to her, she started throwing up and screaming.

I called our veterinarian immediately. Dr. Altman said nandina are poisonous to animals and told me to bring her in at once. Buttercup cried the whole fifteen miles to his clinic. Tyler, Lauren, and I were all about in tears by the time we made it to Dr. Altman, who then quickly proceeded to pump out her stomach. Buttercup survived, but I guarantee you that she never ate nandina again. We learned that day that goats can't eat everything!

We sure enjoyed our years with Buttercup. She gave birth to a pair of beautiful little briar goats and became the most hilarious character of the barnyard, entertaining us all well into her old age.

Five years later, when Tyler was thirteen and Lauren was eleven, the phone rang again after supper one night. It was one of our good friends, Bob Jordan. "I've been doing some thinking. I know you won't be able to take Buttercup with you when you move in a few weeks. We've got some extra room on our farm for an old goat. What do you think about us taking her?"

I smiled, remembering how this story began years before when I had told another farmer, "Okay, I'll take her."

TAKE A MINUTE TO MUSE . . .

We all need help at some point or another. Friends are not luxuries in life; they are necessities. I can still hear my mom telling me, "Lauren, to have a friend, you've got to be a friend. It's as simple as that." The not-so-simple part, though, is actually learning how to be a *good* friend, a friend worth wanting, and a friend worth keeping. Friendship requires sacrifice, skillful communication, unconditional love, nonjudgmental acceptance, and the ability to create a place where "the freedom to stay" or "the freedom to go" both exist in the same corner. Learning how to be a good friend isn't something your children can just read in a book—they learn it by you modeling friendship in front of them and with them. At the same time, I can also hear my mom's voice in my head saying, "Well, I'm not your friend. I'm your parent." It's a fine line that every parent has to learn to toe.

Instead of trying to be the "friend" to them that goes along with every wishful request, or instead of trying to be the "parent" that demands "my way or the highway"—focus more on building a heart-to-heart connection between the two of you. A connection where you're speaking your love to your children in a way they each individually hear and understand. A connection where you teach them how to speak love to you and to your spouse in a language you individually hear and understand. A connection that is so important that reconnection takes first priority any time you become disconnected.

The beauty of it is, instead of wearing yourself out trying to control your toddler or teenager, you'll soon realize that your child will actually begin to make some pretty great decisions. His decisions will be steered solely by his desire to maintain the rich connection you've created. In the face of decisions, he will consider how his choices will affect your heart and the solid friendship you've built. He will be guided by internal motivation instead of the fear of punishment.

- How have your children seen you sacrifice, communicate clear boundaries, unconditionally love, or create the freedom of choice in the friendships you have created with other adults?
- How can you develop your child's skills in this area with their current peer relationships?
- Do you know which "love language" your child speaks and hears most predominantly? (If you haven't read

Dr. Gary Chapman's books *The Five Love Languages* or *The Five Love Languages of Children*, consider adding those to your list.)

- Do you know which "love language" your spouse speaks and hears? (They're often different languages, believe it or not!)
- What are three specific ways you will strengthen your heart-to-heart connection this week?

CREATE YOUR OWN FOREVER WILD EXPERIENCE . . .

The positive, creative ways we play and work beside our children can build strong, confident people at an early age. You can teach your children how to be a generous friend and have the competence and the confidence to "lend a hand" when one of their friends calls for help.

Let me see if I can illustrate this. A class of second graders arrived at Playcard Environmental Education Center for a day of outdoor learning. One of their classmates was in a wheelchair, so we transferred her to our recently acquired golf cart and headed down the trail. We were all having a great day until the golf cart stopped running.

Having had the golf cart only one week, I knew nothing about how to fix it yet. Even though we had all mothers for chaperones, I thought I'd try my luck and ask if any of them knew anything about how to fix an electric golf cart. The mothers shook their heads in unison with a resounding "no, not me."

Just about when we thought we were stuck, I recognized the younger brother of one of my son's best friends. As a family we had spent time together on their tobacco farm. I asked the class of students if there were any more boys that lived on a farm. Two more hands went up.

Without hesitation and with a whole lot of hope, I asked, "Hey, could you three boys please come take a look and see if you can safely get this cart going?"

They confidently walked over to the golf cart, flipped the seat back, pulled on some wires, and asked if I had any tools. One fellow said he had a cart just like this on his farm and that his Dad had taught him how to keep it running. It was now his vehicle.

"Mrs. Roper," I asked, "could you please go back up to the Center with these boys. The toolbox is on the floor in the prep room. Please let them get whatever they need. I'll send the rest of the class on to complete the scavenger hunt while Maggie and I sit here on this log and wait for the teams to come back."

Wouldn't you know, the boys drove the cart to us in less than an hour! I was so thankful. It would have been impossible to maneuver a wheelchair where we were in the woods. Those second-grade farm boys were my heroes. And through that problematic opportunity, they learned that day what it feels like to be a hero.

- If you raise a child in an environment where they are needed and they know there will be no one coming behind them to do what you asked them to do, they will learn to be resourceful, creative, and confident problem solvers.
- What is a real problem that you can ask your children to help solve?

- How will you develop a toolbox of skills that they can competently and confidently use throughout the rest of their life?
- How will you facilitate a way for your child to be a friend and lend a hand by generously sharing their specific skills?

14

Nigel

when you don't know what to do

L IFE HAD CHANGED. A new superintendent had come
to town and had decided to shuffle the deck of teaching
assignments across the county. I was one of the cards that got
shuffled. After eight years of outdoor adventures as the founding director of Playcard Environmental Education Center, I
was transferred to Conway High School to teach biology and
environmental science. My daily jaunts of running through the
swamp with the children in the nature preserve, creative play
in the recently built Native American village, or agricultural
instruction in the barnyard operation had suddenly come to an
end. Almost instantly I found myself in a portable classroom
with rows of desks, fluorescent lights, and four walls. Creativity
would be essential for this teaching assignment.

Fifty-two of my 140 students had been expelled from school when they were only middle schoolers. The good news was that the district office had decided to group them in classes together and enroll them back in high school with the hopes of giving them another shot at a diploma.

It's funny how what often seems to be our most challenging obstacle turns out to be our most exciting source of adventure. After a short while in the classroom I quickly realized that many of my students could not read, much less comprehend a biology textbook. So instead of a textbook, I designed an experiential learning laboratory and created a hands-on method for my students to discover what was written on those textbook pages. And as you might imagine, every good experiential learning laboratory requires critters.

The easiest way to teach with live critters was to set up similar habitats at home and at school, and just transport the animals back and forth on the weekends. By now our children had bottle-fed, incubated, or bathed just about every critter that I had in the learning laboratory at school, so for them it wasn't a big deal. My husband had become a master problem solver and could find a solution to every challenge we faced. He diligently helped me take care of just about any wild beast no matter how slimy or furry it was. The one I had to watch was Miss Josephine, our children's caregiver. I knew it was going to be fun when during her first week of work she showed up with a big jug of turpentine and made sure to saturate every exterior wall of our brick home. To say the least, snakes were not invited guests when she was there.

Nonetheless it was Friday, and we would be home with the children over the weekend, so I picked up my "teaching assistant"

Nigel (my ball python) and put him into an old pillowcase to take him home for his quiet escape. And almost as soon as we got there, it seemed like it was time to go back to school again.

This Monday morning was one of those cold and rainy winter mornings when you wish you could just roll back over and stay in bed. It's on mornings like these that you remember *you* are the adult and somehow find a way to encourage your children to get out the door on time. Tyler, Lauren, and I piled into the station wagon, critters and all, and headed for the schools. Birney went the opposite direction.

After the goodbyes to all the critters and finally to me, the kids jumped out of the car and did the three-legged race under the umbrella, Tyler clinching Lauren to his hip so they wouldn't both get soaked before they got into the school. Next I was on my way to set up before the high schoolers arrived.

Driving past the IGA and the city park, I noticed that we hadn't had a rain like this in a while. Some of the streets were even flooded and traffic seemed to be worse than ever this morning. We all crept slowly along, careful not to get in a wreck.

All of a sudden my car stalled out. I was right under the traffic light and blocking an entire intersection. Not two seconds later and I was thinking about our warm, snuggly bed again and wondering why I'd ever made the decision to get out.

Something major must have malfunctioned because I couldn't even get the motor to turn over. (This was years before any of us had mobile phones, so I felt like I was up the creek without a paddle.) After many attempts to crank it and several frustrated honks from the other drivers in a rush to get to work, a large city police officer appeared at my window and demanded through the glass, "Move your car. You are tying up traffic."

I cracked my window and asked if he could please call a wrecker for me, insinuating that I *had* tried to move my car. I had no idea what might be wrong with it; the car had driven smoothly over the weekend.

That's when he adamantly recommended, "Get out and let me crank this car." Hopeful that he could get it to start, I ran around to the passenger side and jumped back in to get out of the rain. The officer jumped in, moved the seat all the way back and tried the ignition. Almost immediately he started screaming bloody murder and cussing up a storm. But he was paralyzed. His body wasn't moving a muscle, but boy were his lungs! I couldn't imagine what was wrong. At first I thought about the water and wondered if somehow he had gotten electrocuted or hurt by touching the ignition. By the sound of his terror you would have thought he was on fire. I followed his gaze down to his feet, and then I saw the problem. Nigel, my four-foot-long ball python, was crawling across his ankle.

The police officer, still screaming, was literally paralyzed with fear. The color drained right out of his face; he almost turned white in a matter of seconds.

I didn't know what to do. I sure didn't want to claim the snake as my own, but the thought of having a police officer die in my car of a heart attack (with a snake on his foot) was less appealing. So I reached down, grabbed the snake behind the head, and pulled him out from under the driver's seat.

Shockingly, all I heard was the pitter patter of the rain drops. The officer didn't make a sound when I was pulling the snake out. I thought he was holding his breath, but maybe he was just too scared to breathe. When I got Nigel on my side of the car, he opened the car door, had a war with my steering wheel, jumped out in the rain, and then pulled his pistol.

"I ought to shoot that snake and arrest you," he yelled.

I won't repeat his expletives.

"Get out of that car. Stand over there on that sidewalk and hold that snake up over your head so I can keep an eye on it."

As I was loading the car that morning, I had put Nigel in a pillowcase and tied up the end as usual. Somehow when the officer scooted the seat back, the pillowcase must have come untied and, well, Nigel is a professional escape artist. So here I stood on the sidewalk, holding up a snake, soaking wet in a major traffic jam, late for school, and no way to call Birney for help. On top of that, the car wasn't making any progress and my officer friend's nerves were shot.

That's when the thought entered my mind: "Hey, maybe one of my buddies will come by, see me standing here in the rain, and give me a ride."

Right about then, one of my friends passed by; she stopped, rolled down her window, and drove away just as soon as she understood that the snake and I needed to go to school together. A few minutes later it was déjà vu with another friend. At that point there wasn't a dry spot on my body, and I was freezing and beginning to lose heart. I didn't know who I felt like more: Moses with his hands in the air or the traveler in the parable of the Good Samaritan.

"If only the police officer would give me Nigel's pillowcase; I could hide this snake," I thought to myself. But he was too mad. The wrecker came quickly and took my car. Before I could move an inch, the officer left.

Still standing on the side of the road, now with Nigel by my side instead of over my head, my Good Samaritan came by—for the second time. The mother of one of Tyler's baseball buddies had felt bad for not picking me up and had decided to circle the block. When she saw that I was still there, she slowly pulled up beside me and succumbed to her compassionate heart, "Sit in the back seat, Twig. Just don't let me see that snake and maybe I can make it to the high school!"

I thanked her immensely and changed the subject to baseball as if to ignore the very fact I had a python in her back seat.

What a way to start a morning! The students had a good laugh. Nigel kept his head. And by the time the bell rang to go home, I had finally dried out. Funny, how sharing that snake experience seemed to open the lines of communication with some of my students.

TAKE A MINUTE TO MUSE . . .

Sometimes as a parent you find yourself in situations where you just don't know what to do. And sometimes you don't have the time or the opportunity to ask for help. Welcome to parenthood. It's just a part of the party.

Your commitment to personal development and continual growth will be both refreshing and equipping as you journey from diapers to dating with your children. Just as war veterans have a deep comprehension of the reality of their experience each time they share their stories, parents who gather to share their failures, successes, and wisdom often leave feeling inspired, motivated, and understood. Choose your friends wisely. Surround yourself with parents who are positive and intentional about grooming their children to not only survive but to thrive in the days ahead.

And especially on the days when you're standing on the side of the road in the rain with a snake in your hands—try to enjoy the journey along the way. Somehow you live through another day, and in some wild way things inevitably work out.

CREATE YOUR OWN FOREVER WILD EXPERIENCE . . .

A Rotten Log Treasure Hunt

- Take your children on a hike in a forest. The forest floor is covered with fallen trees, branches, and other decomposing vegetation, especially in more humid areas.
- Look for a rotten log. A decaying log is an ecosystem. The log is home to many species of fungi, plants, insects, and other invertebrates.
- If you're lucky, you may see that it is the home of some reptiles, amphibians, and small mammals. Even if they're not "home" at the time, you can identify their presence by the evidence of activity such as chewing patterns, claw marks, tunnels, scat, eggs, tracks, patterns of holes drilled by a bird, etc.
- It makes the treasure hunt more exciting when you put gloves, tweezers, a pocket knife, a magnifying glass, and field guides in your backpack for the hike. Field guides on insects, fungi, mosses, amphibians, reptiles, and mammals speed up your detective work.
- Now the fun begins. When you find your log, be careful not to kick it away from you. Instead roll the log toward

yourself so the snakes move away from you rather than toward you. If you need a lever, use a stick to roll it.

- Wear gloves. Watch out for biting and stinging animals.
- Try not to completely tear up this fragile ecosystem. See how many organisms you can identify using the field guides.
- We like to play with the eyed click beetles and the horn beetles. They have unique behavior patterns.
- We think it is fun to draw, label, and date the biological treasures we find in our "backyards." As you continue to visit your log, you'll be amazed to watch how the decomposers will continue to change the rotten log.
- And don't forget to carefully roll the log back into place before you go as this rotten log is the home of many inhabitants.
- Your children will enjoy being biological detectives. Teach them how much fun it is to discover the answers to their questions.
- Did you ever think a rotten log treasure hunt could be so much fun?

15

Ducklings and Horses
life lessons in hatching and dying

A S A PARENT, one of the worst fears you have is burying your child before you die. Throughout the journey of parenting, whether it's when they are toddlers and you're teaching them to hold your hand as you cross a busy street or when they are teenagers and you're lying in bed at night anxiously awaiting their arrival before curfew, there is always a subconscious question whether they'll make it safely through another day. Life is delicate. With that reality comes the difficult challenge of teaching your child the value and fragility of life, without instilling a paralyzing fear that leads them to paranoia or dependency. Even more demanding is answering the incessant questions about life after death and explaining the confidence we have in eternity.

Not surprisingly, life has its own creative way of teaching us these lessons.

It had already been twenty-seven days and the eggs were about ready to hatch. Lauren, our eleven-year-old daughter, had been meticulously tending to the eleven mallard duck eggs in the incubator on her bedroom floor. Each morning she would jump out of bed to rotate the eggs before school, spraying them down with a cool mist of water as she spoke sweetly to the growing ducklings inside. A nest of eggs had been abandoned on our neighbor's property, and our neighbors had asked us to try to incubate the eggs to see if we could salvage the life that had been started. Birney and I agreed that it would be a powerful lesson of responsibility to let Lauren incubate the eggs and care for the ducklings.

I'll never forget when the first one started hatching. It was early one Saturday morning when we were all asleep. Lauren heard an egg wobbling across the wire bottom of the incubator and some soft peeps. Moments later the whole house was awakened by Lauren's joyful shout, "Daddy, Momma, Tyler, come quick! The ducklings are hatching!"

Birney and I looked at each other and smiled, happy to hear the excitement in her voice but reluctant to part from the cozy bed a few hours too early. When we got to her room, the duckling's egg tooth had made itself visible through a small hole in the wider end of the egg. We all watched in amazement. Little by little the duckling chiseled away at the seemingly thick shell that encased him. It was an arduous struggle for life. The egg would wobble first, followed by an agonizing peep from the duckling as he forced another sliver of the shell away. Slowly and painstakingly the duckling chipped away at the egg until his head finally popped out. The struggle continued until the wings were free and then the entire soaking wet body finally lay free of the eggshell. The duckling was utterly exhausted. I had a deep sympathy for his fatigue, recalling the unforgettable childbirth experiences of our two children. Before long, there was another egg wobbling in the incubator. Duckling number two had also decided that today was a good day to hatch.

Tyler and Lauren were hunched down over the eggs with their faces just centimeters away, watching every move the little ducklings made. After a while Birney and I headed to the kitchen to start breakfast and the impending Saturday morning chores. Tyler soon followed, eager to get outside and play baseball in the yard with his neighborhood friends. But Lauren was entranced. She stayed at the incubator nearly all day, watching as one duckling after another made its debut into the world.

She lined the bottom of a cardboard box with newspaper and hay, clipped a lamp to the side for warmth, and put the chick feed and water dispenser in one corner. The ducklings looked almost lifeless as their wet, exhausted bodies focused on recovering from the strenuous hatching process.

Soon the last egg had begun the journey. Lauren noticed the first break of the shell, the wobbling, and the struggle to crack open. In her excitement, she decided to speed up the process and help the last one come out sooner. He would push and wobble, make that excruciating peep, and just barely peck a small piece of the egg away. Then Lauren took a turn and peeled away another small section of the shell. I was in the laundry room folding clothes when the last one was hatching. Lauren was on her own with this one.

It wasn't until after the duckling was completely out that Lauren realized something was wrong. She moved him over to the warm cardboard box to let him dry off and start eating, but noticed that he looked different from the others. She got scared when he tried to stand up and kept falling over. That was when she called me, "Mom! Something is wrong with my duckling! He can't stand up by himself, and all the other ducklings can."

Perplexed and not sure what to do, I asked her, "Did anything abnormal happen during his hatching process?"

Not knowing that her loving efforts were the exact cause of his deformity, she replied, "Well, I got so excited when he finally started to hatch. I couldn't take hearing that painful peeping sound anymore, so I decided to help him come out. I helped him peel away his shell. He peeled a piece and then I peeled a piece."

My heart ached as she gave her answer because I knew we wouldn't be able to fix him now. One of life's painful lessons was about to be learned, the hard way.

My mind reached for the words to explain it to Lauren delicately, aware of her good intentions. "Lauren, I am afraid this duckling might not make it," I said. "The sound you heard when it was struggling to break open the egg might have been a hard sound for you to hear. I know that it was very hard to watch your duckling struggle on his own. But that struggling process is actually the very thing that makes him strong enough to live outside the egg. The way a duckling cracks open an egg is by using all his strength to push against the wall of the egg with his legs and wings while he knocks the inside of the shell with his egg tooth. It's through that long and tiring process that the duckling's muscles get strong enough to stand up outside the shell."

Her eyes began to water and I could see her putting all the pieces together in her mind. "Oh, Mom, I didn't know. I thought I was helping him. Isn't there anything I can do? I don't want him to die," she cried out through her tears, overwhelmed by the guilt of causing his deformity. I held her close and hoped there was.

Even though she carried him over to the trough and dipped his beak into the water, he was too weak to drink it, or to stand without falling over. A few hours later, he died.

For days we watched our little girl grieve. Her sadness reminded me of a time I had seen a different side of grief on our farm at Playcard Environmental Education Center. We had a barnyard of livestock with every kind of farm animal you could imagine: horses, cows, sheep, goats, pigs, chickens, geese, rabbits, guineas, and ducks—even a donkey and a mule. It was like Noah's Ark. They all lived together in one huge pasture and shared the barn at night. Cocky Locky, our bantam rooster, acted like he was the boss, but every animal knew MoJo, our Tennessee Walker, was the general of the barnyard. MoJo was a gentle twenty-six-year-old chestnut brown horse that everyone liked, including all the barnyard animals.

It was a day when we had scheduled eight kindergarten classes to come out for a morning on the farm. I had gone to work early to make sure everything was ready at the barn and then went back up to the Center to wait for the busses to come. I had just enough time to grab a cup of coffee before they arrived. After we corralled the 240 excited little five-year-olds and separated them out into manageable teams with their teachers and parent chaperones, we all headed to the barn.

On our way over, I heard strange noises coming from the barn. Something was wrong. I couldn't imagine what it was since I had left the barn only thirty minutes ago and everything was in order. I ran ahead of the guests to check it out.

When I got there, I saw MoJo lying lifeless in the large feeding trough. There was a big gash on MoJo's leg where he had hit the side of the trough when he fell. The leg bone was broken and exposed, but there was no blood. His heart must have stopped beating before he fell. Regardless, MoJo was dead and there were 240 kindergarteners walking toward the barn.

That's when I realized MoJo wasn't alone in the trough; he wasn't alone in his death. All the animals in the barnyard had gathered around MoJo's body and were crying. There were baas from the sheep (Rambo and Curly) and goats (Buttercup, Rainbow, and Dewdrop); whinnies from the horses (Pal, Ginger, and Freda); hee-haws from Monroe, the donkey, and Tombstone, the mule. Even Moo Moo, our cow, was mooing.

I knew the students would be at the barn any minute, so I grabbed a couple of picnic blankets and covered MoJo's body. The other horses used their teeth to pull the blankets off of him. Then something amazing happened. They all gathered around and tried to move MoJo as if they were trying to get him to stand up and get out of the trough. They were so upset. I went over to Pal, our Appaloosa stallion. He was quivering all over, twitching as if there were a million flies on him. I had never seen animals grieve like that before, and my heart joined them in the sorrow. I stood there paralyzed, astonished by their sadness and their unyielding desire for MoJo to get up.

That's when I knew that we needed to go ahead and bury MoJo. I ran back up the hill to catch the pack of kindergarteners and explain the dilemma to their teachers, hoping to prevent them from seeing what had happened. The teachers agreed and turned back towards the Center, deciding to roast marshmallows with the children instead, giving us enough time to take care of the pressing priority.

I requested the help of some of the dads in the group and recruited JR off of the lawnmower to come help me at the barn. As quickly as possible, we moved the animals to another pasture and decided to bury MoJo in a nearby field where they could not enter. The animals gathered together as close to the fence as they could and mourned as they watched us dig the grave with a backhoe. Their cries were a song of agony and sadness.

At dinner that night, I shared the story with Lauren. She connected immediately with the sadness the animals had expressed, and she cried as we led her through the process of forgiving herself for what she had done.

In about two days, life appeared to be back to normal in our barnyard, but I knew the animals' sorrow would come and go. And our little girl, like the barnyard animals, turned her attention once more to loving and caring for the other ducklings that were alive, now that she was free through forgiveness.

I learned that day that even the animals grieve. They're sad too and miss their friends when they die. But we also learned a lesson that was just as important: sometimes life doesn't begin again until you learn how to forgive yourself.

TAKE A MINUTE TO MUSE . . .

One of the hardest lessons to endure as a parent is learning that sometimes when you think you're helping the most, you might actually be crippling your child from learning an essential process of natural development. Just as Lauren heard the duckling's agonizing sound as it was struggling to break its way out of the egg and thought she was helping it by reducing its struggle, we can easily think that it is a good thing to step in and use our adult knowledge, power, or experience to shorten the struggle for our children. In a very few instances it may be the best decision. But more often than we'd like to admit, the struggle and the fight to overcome obstacles is the very experience that will create the tension, pressure, and skill development for our children's legs to be strong enough to stand "outside the egg."

- Think of a time when your parents allowed you to struggle and press through the fight to overcome what seemed like an insurmountable obstacle.
- What did that experience of struggling and fighting through the resistance create in you, or how did it increase your skill, self-perception, and maturity? How are you better off from experiencing the struggle?
- Take a minute to survey the situations unfolding in your life right now. Are you in a moment where the sound of your child's struggle urges you to help "chip away the egg" for them? It's normal, and actually very healthy, to have that desire. Don't beat yourself up about it or minimize it, but acknowledge it for what it is—a desire to keep them from any pain, a desire to protect, and a desire to care for them well.
- Now, in light of that desire, take a minute to stare down that road a little farther. Get a good look at your desire to teach them how to think, how to overcome, how to

persevere, how to believe in themselves, how to fight for what really matters. You've got it. You're there. Now, standing in that place, answer this one question: How might your child be different after they push through the resistance and come out on top . . . on their own?

- Do you need to talk with your spouse about the good you see coming from stepping back and encouraging your child to "fight for it" instead of stepping in and rescuing them one more time? If so, set a time to have that talk. Words of confidence in your child's success, ideally coming from both parents, will be the key for them to overcome and unlock the door of their self-doubt. With the key in hand, they're sure to gain the ability to walk through that door and stand on a firm new footing of confidence, skill, and maturity.

CREATE YOUR OWN FOREVER WILD EXPERIENCE . . .

Whether you're an adult or a child, incubating mallard eggs is a most exciting experience. I would encourage you to explore this learning adventure, if possible.

- Obtain an incubator capable of incubating about nine fertilized mallard eggs. (We usually order our eggs through our local feed and seed store but you can also order everything you need online.)
- Follow the specific instructions that come with that particular incubator, type of egg, etc.

- Also study the specific instructions for candling, misting, turning, the hatching process, feed, watering, drowning precautions, etc.
- Ask your child to do all the research, and take advantage of the great conversations that are possible as you prepare for the different stages of development.
- Ask your child to record their discoveries in a journal or scrapbook, or in some other creative form.
- Take time to discuss precautions that could save the life of their little duckling, but then trust them with the process and let the learning begin. (For example: don't buy medicated chick feed, because it will poison the baby duckling. Only buy unmedicated chick feed.)
- It usually takes around twenty-eight days in the incubator before the eggs hatch.
- When you hear the first peeps, it creates as much excitement as Santa Claus.
- Please make sure everyone understands imprinting. The first moving objects the new hatchling sees will become "its mother." If you move, the duckling moves, and will try to run up under you as it would instinctively do with its mother. When you speak, it will try to peep or quack depending on how old it is. Imprinting is a phenomenon that only happens with a few animals.
- Ducklings are defenseless. You (or your child) will have to assume the role of its protector.
- This is a great project to share with your child's schoolteacher. You can help out in advance by thinking of ways to incorporate the other children into the learning. Your

child will love being the "momma duck" and showing off his or her trail of ducklings at school.

- You'll need to locate a pond where other ducks live after about four to five months for their home as adults.
- KEEP YOUR CAMERA NEARBY!

16

Opossum
normal is relative

NOT ALL BEGINNINGS are as they seem. Though all mammals, opossums included, come from a single fertilized egg cell, life after conception gets unique amongst the species. One such beginning is worthy of mention.

Baby opossums are born just twelve to thirteen days after conception. Instead of being carried to term inside the mother's body as we are, opossums spend the rest of their gestation period inside their mother's external pocket, or pouch, like all other marsupials. At birth the baby opossum is about the size of a bumble bee (less than half an inch) and weighs only about 0.1 gram. With neither sight nor hearing as a guide, the newborn opossum instinctively crawls into the mother's pouch to attach to one of twelve or thirteen nipples. Life emerges within a challenge. As many as twenty-six opossums could be born, but since the mother has just twelve or thirteen nipples, only the first half of the litter has a chance to live. Survival of the fittest begins.

The lightweight newborns are able to hold on tightly to their mother by nursing; the swelling nipple and his sucking mouth enables him to stay securely attached, feeding and growing for about three months. They are warm and safe inside the pouch, protected from the world outside their custom-made home. The mother can open and close her pouch to take care of the babies. When the pouch is closed, the mother can even go take a swim without a drop of water ever touching the babies. Now that is some design!

After sixty to seventy days of nursing and growing in the protected pouch, the pups begin to open their eyes and leave the pouch for brief periods. At about eighty to ninety days old, when the pups are six inches long including the tail, they begin to ride on their mother's back and are almost ready to be weaned. You'd never believe that one of the most unique looking creatures that crawls on this earth starts with such a well-fitting beginning.

I got a call one night from my friend Stacey, who had just seen an opossum get hit in the road. She and her two children, Ellie and Jonathan, stopped to see if they could help the animal.

Stacey knew opossums were famous for playing dead, but when she saw the blood coming from its ears and mouth, she knew it had a bad head injury. While they stood there trying to figure out what to do, it died. But within seconds they discovered the movement in her belly and opened the pouch to find five uninjured baby opossums clinging on for dear life. They were so tiny and certainly too young to be weaned.

So without hesitation they placed the babies in an extra tee shirt in the car and headed for home to call the vet. Stacey and her family had rescued orphaned animals before so they knew what to do. They kept them warm and patiently nursed the pups through their development period with a medicine dropper and plenty of fluids. When I saw them, all five of the pups looked healthy and had graduated to a diet that included some solid foods. They had by now become family pets, but when they hissed and showed their sharp pointed teeth they didn't seem so domesticated anymore.

Nonetheless, Stacey generously brought Ellie and Jonathan and their five pups to Playcard occasionally and let the visiting school classes have the rare experience of observing baby opossums. It was always a riot to watch the schoolchildren scream and squirm when they first saw the creatures up close. (For safety reasons, as with all wild animals, the opossums were held so that no one could be bitten or scratched.) The long, pointed face with a pink snout and small eyes was a combination they hadn't seen in their barnyard books. The hairless rat-like tail was a shocking contrast to the coarse gray and white fur. With an opposable thumb-like toe on each hind foot, the opossums couldn't outrun the kids, but by the same token, the kids could never climb as high as the opossums.

After so much fun with the children at the Center, Stacey and I talked about using the opossums to teach a children's church lesson at our church in Conway, thinking that it would be a fun way to show the kids how uniquely God designed His creation. A few weeks later we were up at the front of the church with about thirty children covering the steps. The preacher and choir director were nicely dressed in suits and seated in the large chairs in front of the choir loft behind us. The congregation perked up as they saw the little creatures come out of the bag. Everything went as planned. With the full attention of the children and the adults, we discussed the miraculous ability of our Master Designer to create life and how unique He has made each one of us. The more we study our shy opossum friend, the more convinced we are that only God could make an opossum.

The curious questions from the children were especially hysterical that day. Ellie and Jonathan introduced the opossums and let the other children see the pups up close. The children were amused by how the opossums could hang upside down on Ellie and Jonathan's clothes. After a while I asked the children if they would close their eyes and join me in thanking the Lord for the miracles of life all around us.

When we finished praying and opened our eyes, all of the pups had crawled up into Ellie's hair. This was the end of children's church, so Ellie and Jonathan just got up off the rostrum with the other children, who all started walking back to their parents seated throughout the congregation. But the whole congregation gasped and started scooting down the pews, away from the mob of children. Stacey, the mother, recognized the fear that was spreading, so she calmly walked forward, met her children in the aisle, and began removing the baby opossums from Ellie's hair and placing them in a carrier. It was one of those moments that seem to go in slow motion. Everyone was staring and the order of worship was slightly delayed. Ellie had learned this was the way baby opossums traveled with their moms, so for her it was normal not to carry them in her hands.

That was the day we all learned "normal" is relative.

TAKE A MINUTE TO MUSE . . .

"Normal." What is normal, anyway? Normal for you is what's repeated over and over in your life so that it doesn't seem out-of-the-ordinary until you're exposed to someone else's normal. After a while of encountering so many different normals, you build an increasing understanding of who you are and who you are not, what you like and what you don't like, what you believe and what you don't believe, and likewise see the differences in those around you. Hopefully as adults we have learned to see the value in people themselves and have grown in our ability to separate appearances of status, wealth, or intelligence from the true value of the person. It's always fascinating to watch this progression with children. Peer pressure and a cultural emphasis on clothing style, status objects, and appearing "cool" takes shape in their little minds quicker than we ever imagine.

Whether it's wearing your Crocodile Dundee hat to your daughter's parent-teacher conference or sporting your best pair of black socks with those new white sneakers, learning to be comfortable in your own skin and not think so much about what other people think of you is a liberating secret to parenthood. It's also a secret that will liberate your children as they journey through life, better learned at a young age so they can enjoy years of freedom and fun.

If this is a lesson you've noticed that your children could still profit from learning, have fun with it. Try a few of these stunts to see how quickly your children embrace their true value—apart from status objects or material means—and learn not to be limited by what others might think of them.

- Instead of forking out another hundred dollars for the "trendy" outfit, introduce them to the fun of seeing how far that same hundred dollars can go at a thrift store.
- Next time they sheepishly say, "But, *Mom,* what will the Joneses think?!" smile and intentionally do something to invite them into the joy of facing their fear and tasting confident satisfaction in their identity, just as they are.
- Encourage them to come up with a strategy of how they can earn X amount of money and support them in their endeavors. Let them be the ones to "pitch their idea" to the investor or buyer; let them be the ones to sit on the side of the street and sell their products; let them learn how to overcome their fears and accomplish a goal they believe they can achieve.

CREATE YOUR OWN FOREVER WILD EXPERIENCE . . .

. . . in your own community.

My inspiration to stop and take a look at our little community came from Jay Walljasper's *The Great Neighborhood Book: A Do-it-Yourself Guide to Placemaking.* It is a rich compilation of success stories where people had a common vision of making their neighborhoods nurturing communities. Let's take a moment to discuss how we build community, or a friendly neighborhood. Below are some common activities and examples we share here in Laurens County.

- Look for ways to join others to improve the quality of life in your community. We understand the Greek proverb that a society grows great when old men plant trees whose shade they know they shall never sit in. The families around Clinton, South Carolina, recently planted with the leadership of Clinton High School agriculture students an arboretum with four hundred noble trees (very large native trees) such as the southern magnolia, American beech, willow oak, and live oak to honor our veterans and other community leaders. Our school district didn't have the money to complete all plans for the new high school, so the community took the lead for the arboretum, completing the landscaping for the beautiful new hundred-acre campus.

- Build character in your town. Little details make a difference. Our Clinton High School agriculture students are now in charge of the beautiful plantings in our downtown areas. The touch of color and care shown through their greenhouse plants are special details that add character to our town.

- Identify some favorite public places in your county. Visit and enjoy them and talk about them with others.

- Build comfortable community benches and gathering spots in nature. Take time to stroll, to sit down, and to visit with others. Enjoy what you like most about your community: the people.

- Create bike and pedestrian trails and events similar to Flight of the Dove (a fund raiser for Hospice of Laurens County).

- Sponsor farmers' markets and organic vegetable gardens. Our CSA (community supported agriculture) organic garden, Daniel Parson's Produce, is such fun and very

educational, as Daniel is always teaching us how to cook
and eat the unique variety of vegetables that he grows.

- Keep the teenagers actively involved in projects
that improve their neighborhoods. Our CHAMPS
(Communities Helping, Assisting, Motivating Promising
Students) camps, Boy and Girl Scouts, church youth
groups, YMCA group ministry teams, and school service
organizations are active and needed in building and
strengthening our future community.

- Try to develop community pride through evening con-
certs, block parties, and other special downtown community events. Civic organizations are vital to healthy
communities.

- Celebrate your local hangout—a place where everybody
feels welcome and can easily strike up a conversation with
their neighbor. Find fun ways to welcome newcomers
to your town.

- Continue to introduce new activities that meet community needs, such as a soup kitchen, a united ministries'
food bank, free medical clinic, etc.

- Bring your creative ideas, businesses, and entrepreneur
spirit to your community. Your idea might be the answer
to a genuine problem in your area, or your business
might become the catalyst of rejuvenation within your
community.

- Lastly, teach kindness. We try to teach our children to
be friendly and hospitable. We start with a smile and a
wave. We say hello, and others return the greeting.

- The more of ourselves we invest into our community,
the more it truly becomes home.

17

Deuce
the value of a life

I T WAS HIS FIRST KILL. Richard and Birney pulled up to the house in the truck. Tyler and his cousin Ryan were in the back with the deer. Since it was Thanksgiving weekend, all the women were in the house talking and making the preparations for the big meal. The men had gone deer hunting, and our son Tyler had shot his first buck.

He was soon to experience his initiation into manhood. After we all had a chance to see the deer and remark on its size, the men loaded back into the trucks and set out for the packing shed to go dress out the deer. Call it barbaric, but it is a tradition in our family to smear the deer's blood on the face of the one who just killed it. Whether it's the warm blood on your skin or the savage smell that doesn't seem to leave your nostrils for days, the young man who killed his first deer gets a face-to-face encounter with the finality of his actions. The deer becomes more than just a target. The young hunter finally feels how irreplaceable the life was that he just took.

Something changes in the heart of a hunter on his first kill. There is a value of life that can't be understood until you realize you can't put it back together again. I had learned this lesson myself on the hunts with my dad. It's a lesson that can only be understood through experience; not hearing about it or reading about it—but actually feeling it. I knew it was a lesson our son needed to learn if he was going to grow to be a mature hunter.

When they all came back for supper, Tyler's "bragging story" had turned to a sincere recount of the dressing out techniques he had just learned. Instead of bragging about killing another deer again soon, he was bragging about how much deer meat he conserved and how he learned to dress it out the proper way. It was evident that the life lesson had been learned. His dad, uncles, and granddaddy had done their job well. They taught him respect for the gun in his hands and the significance of the longstanding rule "if you kill it, you eat it." Tyler continued to grow in his hunting skills, bringing home several deer each season to restock my freezer.

A few years later, it was our daughter's turn to learn the value of a life. Lauren was in the ninth grade and Tyler now in the eleventh. The men were preparing for the annual Thanksgiving hunt and were out back getting their rifles loaded into the trucks. Tyler was in the yard putting his legs through a camo jumpsuit. That's when Lauren ran out the back door and hollered, "Hey, can I go hunting with you guys this time?" She had been before, but this time she wanted to hunt. We were all kind of expecting it when she had successfully completed a hunter education class back in middle school and had decided to purchase a hunting license earlier that year; it was just a matter of time.

They all looked to Birney to decide, and when her dad started walking towards the house, it was an understood yes. He went back into the house and got another rifle for Tyler to use. Since he hadn't planned on going this time, and since Tyler was a good shot now, he walked over to Tyler and exchanged guns. "Here, you shoot this rifle. I'll give the rifle with the scope to your sister. You two sit in the stand together so she doesn't get hurt out there by herself." Tyler nodded in agreement and took the gun, confident that everything would be all right.

Birney walked back over to Lauren and gave her the rifle and bullets. He had shown her how to shoot it several times before, but this time was different. She wouldn't be shooting clay skeet today. He told her to be careful and to sit with Tyler in the stand. After she changed into briar britches, a brown turtleneck and camo hat, they all piled in the trucks and were gone within a few minutes.

When they returned a few hours later, we heard the story. Tyler and Lauren had been in the stand for what seemed like hours. It took all the willpower Lauren had to keep quiet for that long, but somehow she endured. They hadn't seen a thing, just a few squirrels playing on the tree below them and a few birds flying right at eye level to them in the stand. It was dusk and starting to get dark when they finally saw a deer. Way off across the soybean field, about 125 yards from their stand, a large eight-point buck stepped out from the wood's edge into the clearing. Tyler elbowed Lauren to look.

They both just sat there for a while, staring at it. He was a huge buck. Lauren put her scope on him to get a view up close.

Tyler squinted his eyes and sat very still. With the scope Lauren could see the details of his body. His muscular neck bent down to eat some soybeans off the ground. He would lift his head every now and then, cautiously scanning the horizon for danger. But Tyler and Lauren were so far away and hidden in the tree, he couldn't pick up their scent yet.

Tyler pressed his finger on the safety to take it off and looked at Lauren as if to say, "Well, are you ready or are you just going to sit there?" Lauren could hear her heart beating in her ears. Tyler whispered, "Okay, on the count of three, we're both going to fire." Lauren was steadying the rifle on the board in the stand. Her heart had been racing, but as soon as he gave the instructions she got buck fever. Her hands started shaking so bad she almost dropped the gun. Tyler knew he couldn't wait long or she'd shake her way out the tree. The next thing Lauren recalls hearing is "two, one, bang." Somehow "three" was never mentioned. The two guns fired as close to simultaneous as possible. Lauren had her scope on him and could see the deer fall to the ground immediately. She said he kicked once before he stopped moving. And then it was over. The buck was down.

Still shaking and with a racing heart, Lauren followed Tyler down out of the tree stand, careful not to drop the rifle in the dirt. It was getting darker by the second. They had heard other gunfire off in the distance and knew their cousins were in stands in other parts of the field. It was safe for them to get down and find the buck.

The deer seemed even bigger when they got to him. Lauren rubbed her hand down his still warm back and felt his bristly hair in between her fingers. She touched his wet nose and saw the deer ticks covering his ears. From the way she told the story, it seemed like it was his eyes that really got her. His deep black eyes were still open and seemed to express his sudden surprise encounter with death. It didn't take bloody war paint to connect the dots for Lauren; her tender feminine heart understood quite well. Standing right there in the field with that buck, her heart and mind learned the lesson—she had taken his life and couldn't bring it back again.

Tyler gave her a few minutes. He knew exactly what she was thinking about. Then he started really looking and feeling around for the bullet holes. After searching his whole body over, they only found one hole. It had gone straight into his heart making it a good shot and a quick death.

We joke that Lauren got him with the scope. Tyler played along with it, as it was one of many deer that he had dropped. Nonetheless, the rack of antlers is fashionably memorialized at our home with a plaque bearing the deer's name. Tyler and Lauren affectionately refer to him as "Deuce."

TAKE A MINUTE TO MUSE . . .

As children age, the encounters with risk and responsibility naturally get bigger. As parents age, we hope our children have learned the lessons of self-control and wisdom when they were young—very young—especially when we put a gun and a box of shells into the hands of our teenager. I know, you are probably thinking, "What kind of a parent does that?!"

The truth of the matter is you can't control a two-year-old any more than you can control a teenager. The "I'll give you something to cry about" society tries to make us think we can, but you soon realize, as you count way past three, that your son or daughter has already calculated the cost of the spanking and *still* chooses to disobey.

The great day arrives when you finally come to terms with the liberating reality that controlling your two-year-old or controlling your teenager is in fact *not* your job as a parent. Believe it or not, it's their job. It's your job to teach them how to make good decisions with the choices that are before them. It's their job to learn to control themselves, as children, as teens, and as self-sufficient adults. Even God himself doesn't try to control us humans. After all, it was God who put *both* the "tree of good and evil" and the "tree of life" in the garden, way back when. For love to exist there must be an environment of free will: *the ability to choose* love over evil, *the ability to choose* to be connected to someone or to separate yourself from them.

Moreover, it is when children are two-year-olds that we get the incessant multitude of opportunities to help them see the two roads before them—option 1 or option 2—and to help them understand the consequences that would befall them (both positive and negative) from choosing option 1 or option 2. Then, we must love them enough to let them choose, experience the consequences of their own choice (as long as they are not in danger), and thereby actually learn from it. Trust me, option 1 and option 2 in a two-year-old's world are much safer to learn from than the options in a teenager's world.

- What is something you find yourself battling your two-year-old or your teenager on, repeatedly?
- What are some options you can help your youngster see that they might not be seeing now because, by force or flattery, you've convinced them to do it your way so far?

- What are some safe ways you can truly let your children experience the consequences of their own decisions, and let the experience of the consequence do the talking for you?
  - □ SIDE NOTE: It is especially important to be mindful of your *words* during this type of vulnerable learning moment. "I told you so" remarks or "see, that's what you get" comments not only unravel the entire teaching process, but they leave destructive and debilitating wounds on your child's heart. Even as an adult those words will haunt them if you don't reconcile.
  - □ Sadly, most of us grow into adulthood without ever learning what it looks like to truly reconcile. Here's a good start. First, take responsibility for the pain you caused them and admit that what you did was wrong. Then stop a moment and really try to understand and feel the pain *they* might be feeling. Tell them what you imagine they are feeling or thinking and allow them to confirm or further explain their experience. This is often the hardest but the most fruitful part—because this is the moment where they feel heard, known, valued, and worth more than the pain you caused them. Now tell them how it makes you feel knowing you caused them this pain. You will be amazed how easy it will be past this point. Your heart will put words in your mouth, because you'll see past the thing that annoyed you, past the part of them that makes you angry—you'll see them as they really are. Next express your genuine commitment to not repeat this wound and, finally,

ask them to forgive you for the harm. It is through this meticulous reconciliation process that bleeding wounds are cauterized and truly healed.

▫ If a wound is bubbling to the surface right now— one of those bleeding, pussy, infected wounds that someone caused you and never bothered to reconcile, or simply didn't know how to reconcile—before you shove it back down in there deeper than before, I invite you to pause with me and consider. How might your life be different if that very wound got healed today? How might you be able to love the person who hurt you, to love yourself, or to love your children in a way that you've always hoped for? How valuable is it to you to pursue healing? (For more information, see *Loving on Purpose* and *Love After Marriage*, p. 167).

⨳ CREATE YOUR OWN FOREVER WILD EXPERIENCE . . .

If you're not a hunter or fisherman, consider learning the skill and teaching your children to be competent and wise hunters. Whether it's the appreciation for wildlife that comes when you eat what you kill or the deep love of the outdoors, it shouldn't come as a surprise that hunters and fishermen do more for wildlife preservation than any other segment of the American population. Check out your state's Department of Natural Resources website to sign up for a hunter education class and learn the ins and outs of firearm safety, the ethics and responsibilities of a hunter, and practical skills for your hunting experience. This course is often required to obtain a hunting license.

Hunting isn't limited to firearms. Archery is a fun activity to teach children. As with all sports, we teach safety practices and supervise as our children are learning. A simple recurve bow, a few wooden arrows with target points, and a large standalone bull's-eye target is all you need. If your child is inspired by a challenge, make a competition out of it and involve all the neighborhood kids. They'll be ready for the Olympics before you know it!

Once you've mastered archery, explore some other fun outdoor activities together as a family. Most state and national parks have access to equipment so you can try the activity without having to purchase the equipment first. Nature-based or historic tourism businesses will also work with you to experiment with a new outdoor activity you haven't tried yet. Some of our favorites in the South are:

- swimming
- canoeing
- rafting
- kayaking
- gardening
- hunting
- fishing
- birding
- butterfly hunts
- nature photography
- racing turtles, frogs, and lizards
- zip lines
- tracking
- geocaching

- horseback riding
- driving horse carts and wagons
- building playscapes and hideouts
- hiking
- biking
- model rocketry
- nature treasure hunts
- free play
- camping
- cooking over a campfire
- boating
- skiing
- shrimping
- crabbing
- flounder gigging
- attracting and watching wildlife
- making music, whether with animal calls or musical instruments

Certainly this list is just a start. Refer to the Outdoor Play Resources list at the end of this book for more resources on the importance and impact of, and limitless ideas for, playing outside.

18

Eely

knowing the way home

SITTING HERE ON THE BED beside my mom as her time
left on this earth is quickly shortening with each shallow
breath she takes, my mind can't help but go back to the experience with dad. I remember it all so clearly . . .

One more tug and the crawfish trap would be up on the
old grits mill dam, the perfect place to see what was in today's
catch. There she was, shimmering in the late afternoon sun.
She looked like a snake, but then I saw the gills and realized it
was the first American eel I'd ever seen in this swamp. Excited
about catching her, I ran back through the trails and inside the
main building at Playcard Environmental Education Center to
prepare a large aquarium for my new friend.

All summer she seemed to be content to swim around in the aquarium water. Her graceful, fluid movement was enchanting to watch. But when fall came, something caused Eely's behavior to change. She would swim around the aquarium as fast as she could, knocking the top off, splashing the water up over the rim, and doing everything in her power to get out. Eely was determined to leave. Thank goodness, the American eel is capable of breathing through its slimy skin as well as its gills and can exist for several hours out of the water. There were a few mornings I got to work and found her on the other side of her aquarium—the dry side.

One afternoon I got a call from the hospital to come in. Dad had gone into the hospital that morning and now they were calling to tell me that he was hemorrhaging, and his doctors couldn't find the bleeder. Tyler was nine and Lauren was seven. They both had lots of questions, as all curious children that age do: "What happens to us when we die? Mommy, where is heaven? How do we get there?"

Somehow, when it's *your* dad that's in the hospital, those questions seem more real than ever, and all the answers you once knew now feel miles and miles away. It was then that God used Eely to help me find some answers to those tough questions our kids had been asking.

I hung up the phone after telling the hospital staff I'd be on my way just as soon as I could get the Center locked up. Fighting back the tears, and hearing those questions in my head again, I walked into the main teaching classroom to see what was going on in the aquarium. Our formerly calm eel was still engaging in the abnormal splashing and intense swimming.

Eely was a female eel that had hatched way out in the Sargasso Sea—between Bermuda and the Azores, right in the middle of the Atlantic Ocean—like all other American eels that swim the coastal rivers of the eastern seaboard. Eely hatched from a tiny egg laid in the salt water and grew into a larva that drifted with the Gulf Stream. Shortly after hatching, she began her journey. As she was growing, she swam all the way across the Atlantic Ocean to Winyah Bay, and then up into the fresh water of the Big Pee Dee River, before making her way into the Little Pee Dee River, the Great Lakes Swamp, the Pleasant Meadow Swamp, and then finally into Playcard Swamp. That's thousands of miles. I knew Eely was a female because the males stay down in the brackish waters at the mouth of the freshwater rivers in the Winyah Bay area.

Her splashing and thrashing about in the aquarium was getting more intense. As I was feeling rushed to get to the hospital to see my dad, and still perplexed by Eely's behavior, it dawned on me that she too was in a rush. It was as if she were fighting the clock. That's when it all made sense. God made eels to instinctively know the exact time when they were to begin their journey all the way back to the Sargasso Sea to spawn and die. American eels can live from ten to forty years in fresh water before returning to spawn.

It's no coincidence that on this day, when my heart needed to be reminded of my Creator and His ability to communicate so clearly with His creation, that Eely fought with all her life to show me the answer.

As I was picking Eely up off the floor and putting her back into the water, it was as if God said to me, "Don't worry about your dad. If I can guide an American eel all the way from Playcard Swamp back to the Sargasso Sea, I can surely take your dad home to be with Me. I love him. I gave My life for him, and he gave his life to Me. Your dad doesn't have to worry about finding his way to heaven."

Before I left for the hospital, I carried Eely back down to the swamp. She knew it was time. I remember walking down the trails towards the water, watching her intensity in the bucket swirling and building with her determination. She had the stamina and the will to make the journey. As I leaned off the edge of the dam, she dove out of the bucket and into the black river water.

I smiled, vicariously absorbed the life, passion, and purpose in that little eel, and walked back through the woods, thanking my God for speaking to me so clearly again today. He gave me so much more than a few words to answer my children's questions; He gave me an encounter with Himself.

Dad checked out for his trip to heaven six years later when Tyler was fifteen and Lauren thirteen. We shared some wonderful times together during those last six years. And we are looking forward to being together again in heaven.

Today, hearing our extended family sing an old hymn to my mom as she leaves her earthly body, I remember those comforting words again and confidently know—she doesn't have to worry about finding her way home.

⏱ TAKE A MINUTE TO MUSE . . .

What about you? What are the questions you still have that are unanswered? Or better yet, what are the questions that you need more than just words to satisfy your heart—those questions that demand an experiential encounter to believe. The first step towards your answer is to ask. You'll never know until you decide to be bold enough, or desperate enough, to ask. Then take deliberate, intentional note of the answer. From my experience, I can tell you that His answer is sure to come.

In our present-day world of medicine, where seemingly limitless technological possibilities make a heart transplant normal, death is starting to feel more and more like an "abnormal" part of life. Our culture dreads the thought of aging, we fight death with every means possible, and we avoid the thought of our journey home until the trip is upon us. Please don't misunderstand; our world is not as "safe" as it used to be when children roamed outside from sunup to sundown, only coming inside for lunch and supper. I understand that we must give prudence and careful thought to the environments and situations in which we allow our children to explore. There is an element, however, of being secure with *the ending* that enables you to *begin living* in a new way. When you recognize that your role as a parent began through a creation that you could have never created on your own, nor could ever recreate in the same way, you realize that there is a level of stewardship that is core to the experience of parenting. You understand that your aim is to do the best job possible loving and caring for a little person who isn't yours to keep forever. Your children are yours for this earthly season of life. It is that paradigm that empowers you to live beyond the fear of death, certainly not in stupidity, but beyond the grip of fear and into the freedom of unshakable love.

·◇· CREATE YOUR OWN FOREVER WILD EXPERIENCE . . .

Today state and national parks are being shut down because of a significant decline in use, a trend that started almost a decade

before the major economic downturn of 2008. You don't have to
be a sociologist to recognize that our younger generation spends
most of its time watching a screen—whether TV, computer,
tablet, or cell phone—and spends a drastically decreased amount
of time in the out-of-doors than its preceding generation. As
adults, if we do not allow for immersion experiences in nature
or create meaningful ways to once again connect our children
with the real, natural world around them, we will propagate
destruction of our planet through the disconnection we've pas-
sively permitted. It is the understanding of our dependency on
nature and a true appreciation and enjoyment of nature that
creates the actual desire to wisely conserve our natural resources.
Unless our children experience a tangible love for our natural
world and personally see the value in its health, they will not
fight to protect it.

So on that note, I challenge you to expand your world of
outdoor experiences, especially with your children.

- Research a place you would like to visit.
- Find a friend to go share it with you and have fun!
- You might even discover some new recreational activities
  in the outdoors that you've always wanted to try.
- How would you design your dream family adventure if
  you could schedule it for next week?
- What were some of your favorite outdoor experiences
  as a kid? How can you help to recreate those for your
  own children?
- What life lessons would you hope to learn through your
  next experience?

In closing, I want to paint one final picture and ask you one final question.

When your bags are packed for your departure from earth . . . when you're lying there looking back on your life . . . and your children are there with you, loving you, touching you, caring for you, and savoring every second face-to-face with you, what are the memories they will be sharing out loud in that room? What are the stories they will tell their children at bedtime? What are the memories that will shape their lives for eternity?

How might your life—and theirs—be different by choosing to be their forever wild parent, today?

The Next Generation

LIFE WAS NEVER BORING at our house. I can remember bullfrog jumping contests in the yard, and betting my peanuts on a box turtle or a slider to win a turtle race; I can remember lying on our bellies shooting marbles down our long wood-floored hallway, or seeing who could make the loudest bicycle using a deck of cards and some of mom's old clothespins. I am learning each year as I get older that my childhood was a rare experience. Not only rare in all the life lessons learned through nature, but rare in the quality and quantity of love that lived so powerfully in our home.

My mom is a hoot. She's the kind of lady that knows how to make chores fun. Her spontaneity and creativity instigated some of the best memories. One of my favorites is the famous lizard race. I can still feel myself holding my breath as we watched a lizard race from my ear to my brother's ear, across a skinny line of string. She has a way of "seizing the moment" for a playful joke, a learning opportunity, or a memory that will stay with you forever. She taught us that, with God, anything is possible. And I mean anything. This book doesn't even touch on some of the "wild" stories of her tangible interactions with God. If I can ever get her to write those down, now that will be a book worth reading!

My dad, as you can clearly tell from the stories, has more kindness and patience than any man on earth. Not to mention, he's absolutely brilliant. He taught me how to ride a bicycle without training wheels by setting up an obstacle course in our yard. Somehow I got so distracted by making it through the next obstacle that I didn't even think about the two absent extremities I once hinged my life upon. He is the most generous person I have ever known. I have watched him diligently care for and sacrificially give to others with the purest altruism; it's a love that chooses to give out of a place of absolute liberty.

Tyler and I grew up like twins instead of siblings separated by two years. He is no doubt one of my best friends. There hasn't been a subject we haven't broached, a question too hard to ask each other, or a dream that hasn't grown every time we get together. Though it felt like we were twins, Tyler has always been my brave older brother. Whether it was sitting in the dentist chair first and letting me watch him get his teeth cleaned while he gurgled comforting words to me, or watching him jump off the rock quarry first when we were teenagers before I worked up the courage to jump myself—there isn't another brother who could have done a better job of protecting me, teaching me, and loving me like Tyler has.

Now, married one year, Todd and I have already started dreaming about the way we want to raise our little warriors one day. Though we're really looking forward to savoring our "just us" years before the children come, we get so excited each time we share stories from our childhood and think of all the creative ways this world can be introduced to those insatiably inquisitive minds, innocent hearts, and faith-filled trust of the little people—what a joy it will be to parent.

My parents grew up in the same hometown, Allendale, South Carolina. They both had their own dose of wild outdoor adventures in their childhood. My dad learned the ropes from his parents, who had moved from Ohio to start a farm down south. My mom was the sidekick to her dad, the agriculture teacher who could do just about anything outdoorsy. Life lessons from nature seem to be the best "hands-on" approach our family knows to rearing children—exposing them to the realities of life's natural consequences while still savoring each unforgettable memory along the way.

What really happened through the way our parents raised us is that they chose to risk: to risk our hearts getting hurt, to risk learning the hard way, and to risk us suffering in the small life lessons so that we'd be wiser and better equipped for the bigger life lessons. They weren't afraid of failure. It is that same courage that still exists in them now as parents of adult children. That courage has enabled them to create an environment of freedom in which we have learned to be powerful people. Love requires an environment of freedom to be able to choose—to choose to love the other person, each of us choosing to take personal responsibility to maintain and enrich the connection between us. Inside these stories and moments of musing, my hope is that you will see the deeper hue of *Forever Wild* PARENTING: intentional love within a family.

Lauren B. Bontrager
daughter of the author

From barefoot summer days spent pulling turtle traps to twilight frog identifying expeditions, my childhood focused on squeezing every last adventure opportunity out of the day. Now, looking back in reflection, I realize how much of an impact the adventures in the swamp played in my life. We all share a common bond; our experiences during childhood play an incredible role in shaping the men or women we become. This book gives a great view into the unique way my parents taught my sister and me and exposed us to the essential lessons of life, death, faith, and perseverance.

Tyler Blind
son of the author

Lauren's Favorite Marriage & Family Resources

I F YOU'RE LOOKING FOR the "best of the best" resources to build the intimate marriage you've always wanted and create the family life that you know is possible, look no farther.

Loving on Purpose
Danny and Sheri Silk
www.lovingonpurpose.com

Love After Marriage
Barry and Lori Byrne
www.loveaftermarriage.org

Deliverance and Wholeness Retreats
Bear Creek Ranch, Portal, Georgia
Tim and Katie Mather
www.bearcreekportal.com

Grooming the Next Generation for Success
Dani and Hans Johnson
www.danijohnson.com

Books
The Five Love Languages | Gary Chapman
Boundaries | Dr. Henry Cloud and Dr. John Townsend
Love & Respect | Emerson Eggerichs
Necessary Endings | Dr. Henry Cloud
Sheet Music | Dr. Kevin Leman
Millionaire Next Door | Thomas Stanley and William Danko
When Heaven Invades Earth | Bill Johnson
Victory over the Darkness | Neil T. Anderson
Bondage Breaker | Neil T. Anderson
Culture of Honor | Danny Silk

Outdoor Play Resources

Cohen, Rebecca P. *Fifteen Minutes Outside: 365 Ways to Get Out of the House and Connect with Your Kids.* Naperville, IL: Sourcebooks, 2011.

Farmer, Charles H. *Sharks of South Carolina.* Charleston, SC: South Carolina Department of Natural Resources Marine Resources Division, 2004.

Keeler, Rusty. *Natural Playscapes: Creating Outdoor Play Environments for the Soul.* Redmond, WA: Exchange Press, 2008.

Lanza, Patricia. *Lasagna Gardening: A New Layering System for Bountiful Gardens: No Digging, No Tilling, No Weeding, No Kidding!* Emmaus, PA: Rodale Press, Inc., 1998.

Louv, Richard. *Last Child in the Woods: Saving Our Children from Nature-Deficit Disorder.* Chapel Hill, NC: Algonquin Books of Chapel Hill, 2008.

Louv, Richard. *The Nature Principle: Reconnecting with Life in a Virtual Age.* Chapel Hill, NC: Algonquin Books of Chapel Hill, 2012.

Soebel, David. *Wild Play: Parenting Adventures in the Great Outdoors.* San Francisco, CA: Sierra Club Books, 2011.

Skenazy, Lenore. *Free Range Kids: How to Raise Safe, Self-Reliant Children (Without Going Nuts With Worry).* San Francisco, CA: Jossey-Bass, 2009.

Walljasper, Jay. *The Great Neighborhood Book: A Do-it-Yourself Guide to Placemaking.* Gabriola Island, BC, Canada: New Society Publishers, 2007.

The Children & Nature Network:
www.childrenandnature.org

Eustace Conway
www.turtleislandpreserve.com

Outdoor play supplies:
- Acorn Naturalists:
  www.acornnaturalists.com/store
- Carolina Biological Supply Company:
  www.carolina.com

Forever Wild Play Days

Come play with us!

Need something fun to do with the grandchildren this weekend? Tired of watching movies and staying inside? Want to make memories with your youngsters that they'll never forget? Then mark your calendar for the next *Forever Wild* PLAY DAY.

Forever Wild PLAY DAYS are just plum fun!

Parents and grandparents bring their children and grandchildren to join us for a one-of-a-kind experience playing together outside. Depending on the time of year and the PLAY DAY location, each experience is planned with unique activities that are sure to make memories you'll never forget.

Check out our website for more information: *www.foreverwildadventures.com*

A few tips to make your PLAY DAY most enjoyable:
- Bring your camera. You'll go home with lots of captured memories.
- Wear comfortable clothes and shoes.
- Wear a hat to keep the sun and bugs out.

Forever Wild Friends

You're invited!

We so value playtime in the great outdoors that we have formed a group of friends called *Forever Wild* FRIENDS. Our *Forever Wild* FRIENDS look forward to playing together and eating a meal together each month at our special events.

Here is just a sampling of our recent adventures:

- Eating a gourmet sunrise breakfast at Musgrove Mill golf course overlooking the Enoree River and then jumping into thirty-five golf carts for a guided ornithology ID hunt on an unbelievably beautiful course along the river.

- Planning a scrumptious pick, cook, and eat adventure at our CSA garden and Irish bed and breakfast, the Farmhouse at Bush River. Fifteen of us gardening buddies worked with three chefs and prepared twelve different dishes. What a fun and delicious meal!

We can hardly wait for the next adventure. The greatest reward for our time invested together in nature is the new friendships we form each month. **You can check our website** for more ideas on how to form a *Forever Wild* FRIENDS group in your area.

And maybe you could even join us on our next adventure here in beautiful South Carolina.

Check out our website for more information:
www.foreverwildadventures.com

Forever Wild Coaching

Create the life you—and your family—desire.

Your life matters—every day of it. Parents understand more than anyone how fast the days go by, how quickly the children grow, and how few moments are left until they're packing their bags for college.

Don't wait until then to create the connection you've always wanted. Join other parents like yourself who are serious about overcoming the obstacles to achieve the vision they have for their family.

Through coaching, you will sharpen your parenting skills in the catalyzing environment of accountability. Individual, couple, and group coaching experiences offer the specific tools to intentionally build the connection within your family that you know is possible.

Check out our website for more information:
www.foreverwildadventures.com

CPSIA information can be obtained at www.ICGtesting.com
Printed in the USA
LVOW06s1415130913

352354LV00002B/2/P